# Pioneers, SHOWMEN AND THE RFC

## EARLY AVIATION IN IRELAND 1909–1914

D1477337

## GUY WARNER

**COLOURPOINT**

Published 2016 by Colourpoint Books
an imprint of Colourpoint Creative Ltd
Colourpoint House, Jubilee Business Park
21 Jubilee Road, Newtownards, BT23 4YH
Tel: 028 9182 6339
Fax: 028 9182 1900
E-mail: sales@colourpoint.co.uk
Web: www.colourpoint.co.uk

First Edition
First Impression

A catalogue record for this book is available from the British Library.

Designed by April Sky Design, Newtownards
Tel: 028 9182 7195
Web: www.aprilsky.co.uk

Printed by W&G Baird Ltd, Antrim

ISBN 978-1-78073-106-3

*Front cover:* Vincent Killowry's evocative depiction of the scene at the inaugural Irish aviation meeting at Leopardstown Racecourse in 1910, which hangs in the Officers' Mess at Baldonnel, Headquarters of the Irish Air Corps.

Rear cover: The unique pioneer Lilian Bland outside the coachhouse at her home, Tobarcorran House, in the village of Carnmoney, Co Antrim, with one of the wings of her aeroplane, the *Mayfly*. It was the first to be designed, built and tested by a woman.
*(via John Sherlock)*

*About the author:* Guy Warner is a retired schoolteacher and former civil servant, who grew up in Newtownabbey, attending Abbots Cross Primary School and Belfast High School before going to Leicester University and later Stranmillis College. He now lives in Greenisland, Co Antrim with his wife Lynda. He is the author of more than 20 books and booklets on aviation and has written a large number of articles for magazines in the UK, Ireland and the USA. He also reviews books for several publications, gives talks to local history societies, etc and has appeared on TV and radio programmes, discussing aspects of aviation history.

# Contents

Harry Ferguson's garage in Belfast in September 1912. His own aircraft and a Blériot are visible. *(ARH-063 © National Museums Northern Ireland)*

# GRAND AEROPLANE EXHIBITION.

## Flying at Castlebar.

### MR. JAMES VALENTINE,

The Famous Aviator, will give EXHIBITION FLIGHTS on his

## MONOPLANE

— IN THE —

## Asylum Grounds, Castlebar,

(By kind permission of the Committee)

# ON TUESDAY NEXT,

### THE 15TH OCTOBER.

Gates will be Open at 2 p.m.  Flying will Commence at 3 p.m.
An Explanation of the Machine and a Demonstration of the uses of its various parts will be given before the Flights.
Admission 1s.  Private Enclosure extra.

### Special Railway Facilities at Reduced Fares.

### CASTLEBAR BRASS BAND WILL BE IN ATTENDANCE.

## Come in Your Thousands
and avail of this rare opportunity.

Tickets on Sale at T. A. WYNNE'S, Castlebar.

# Foreword

In my grandmother's house was copy of Harry Harper's 1948 book *Conquerors of the Air*, bought for my father's 12th birthday. Long forgotten I found it in her attic in the 1980s and the book opened a world for me of American, British and French aviation pioneers who dared to climb into their often dangerous aeroplanes to change the world.

In his new book, Guy Warner shows that Ireland was also a place of pioneers, from gentlemen amateurs to manufacturing professionals. The story of Harry Ferguson is well known but with Guy's usual meticulous research other pioneers are identified, men and women, most hailing from the industrial north of Ireland, which surprised me. Maybe the agricultural economy of southern Ireland seemed to make people reluctant to fly in the years before the First World War.

Nonetheless people did want to see these new pilots and their planes. Air shows, which are a regular event today during the summer, were very popular before the First World War. Ireland's first at Leopardstown Race Course in south County Dublin attracted thousands of people to see the new machines and the brave men who flew them in the summer of 1910. Indeed it is calculated that the Irish public in this period saw aeroplanes in 50 places, spread around 23 counties.

Guy also tackles the debate that there has always been among journalists of the day and aviation historians about who was the first to fly over the Irish Sea, a feat which was completed only three years after Louis Blériot's successful flight over the English Channel in 1912. Finally Guy examines the little known story of the Royal Flying Corps' first visit to Ireland in the summer of 1913 where they flew over 2000 miles as part of the last large British army divisional exercises in Ireland prior to the outbreak of war. Less than a year later the same pilots were fighting in France and were to be joined by 6000 Irish born pilots from 1914–1918.

It is to Guy Warner's credit that he has created another wonderfully produced book, beautifully designed with previously unseen photographs and new research opening another part of Ireland's hidden history. I highly recommend this book to anyone interested in Ireland's twentieth century history.

*Lar Joye*
*Curator of Military History*
*National Museum of Ireland*

*Dublin, October 2016*

**Map of locations from
1909–1914**

Ballycastle

White Strand ☆        Magilligan Strand ☆

Derry/Londonderry ○  ○ Eglinton        Ballymoney
☆ Waterside

Larne

Randalstown
○                           Carnmoney Hill
Masserene Park (Antrim) ☆     ☆    ○ Bangor
BELFAST              ○ Newtownards
Balmoral Show Grounds ☆

Dungannon ○    ○ Lurgan   ○ Hillsborough

Banbridge ○    Dundrum    Ballyhornan ○
Bryansford
Newry ○      ○○ Newcastle
○ Warrenpoint

○ Cavan    Dundalk ○

○ Castlebar

○ Kells    ○ Drogheda
○ Navan

○ Tuam    ○ Mullingar

Phoenix Park    ○ Howth Head ☆
Donadea Castle ☆    ☆ DUBLIN
○ Galway    Leopardstown Park Racecourse ☆

The Curragh (Kildare) ☆    ☆ Bray
Powerscourt

Birr ○
Sharavogue ☆    ○ Maryborough (Portlaoise)
Shinrone ☆    ○ Roscrea

☆ Jenkinstown
Limerick ○    Kilkenny ○    Gorey ○
☆ Rathbane

Fethard ○    ○ Enniscorthy

Clonmel ○    ☆ Kilcash    ○ New Ross
○ Tralee    ○ Wexford
Waterford ○

○ Cork    Youghal ○    | ○ Town/city
| ☆ Other location
Bandon ○

Clonakilty ○

miles
0        25        50        75        100

0        50        100        150
kilometres

Map data: ©MAPS IN MINUTES™/Collins Bartholomew 2007

# Introduction

1909 WAS A MOMENTOUS year in aviation history: in February Eustace Short (1875–1932) made an agreement with Wilbur Wright (1867–1912) to build six Wright aircraft under licence in Britain, on which the claim would subsequently be based that Short Brothers were the first volume aircraft manufacturers in the world; two months later, John Moore-Brabazon (1884–1964) became the first resident Englishman to make an officially recognized aeroplane flight in England on 2 May 1909, at Shellbeach on the Isle of Sheppey with flights of 450 feet (137 m), 600 feet (182 m), and 1500 feet (457 m) in his 60 hp (44 kW) Voisin biplane *Bird of Passage*; in the spring Zeppelin LZ5 made a long distance flight of 39 hours and 39 minutes, covering 712 miles (1150 km), its creator, Count Ferdinand von Zeppelin (1838–1917) became a national hero; on 25 July Louis Blériot (1872–1936) flew across the English Channel in 36½ minutes in a 25 hp (18 kW) Blériot XI; in August the

*Above:* John Moore-Brabazon. *(Author's Collection)*

*Above left:* His Voisin biplane *Bird of Passage.* *(Author's Collection)*

*L-r:* Eustace Short, Wilbur Wright and Count Ferdinand von Zeppelin. *(Author's Collection)*

Louis Blériot sets off across the English Channel on 25 July 1909 completing the journey in 36½ minutes. (Author's Collection)

Louis Blériot sets off across the English Channel on 25 July 1909 completing the journey in 36½ minutes. (Author's Collection)

The official programme of the 'Doncaster Aviation Contest' held in October 1909. (Author's Collection)

first international meeting for aeroplanes was held at Reims[1], following which the Blackpool Aviation Meeting ran from 19–23 October – the first officially recognised air display to be held in the United Kingdom, though this is disputed by Doncaster.

During the course of the next five years piloting an aircraft would become a professional rather than a sporting activity and aircraft design would progress from educated guesswork to progression based on experience and empirical evidence. In the next five years the maximum speed record of 34 mph (54.81 kph) set in 1909 by Paul Tissandier (1881–1945) in a Wright biplane would increase almost fourfold, maximum altitude attained of 508 feet (155 metres) set by Hubert Latham (1883–1912) in an Antoinette monoplane increase to more than 19500 feet (6000 metres) and unrefuelled duration from two hours 43 minutes and 24 seconds, set by Louis Paulhan (1883–1963) in a Voisin biplane, to 21 hours.

Learning to fly was just in process of being established on an organized basis. The Royal Aero Club (RAeC) issued its first Aviator's certificate in March 1910. By the end of the year 45 airmen had qualified to receive this certification (of these 15 had flown from Brooklands in Surrey, six from Eastchurch in Kent and seven from Hendon in North London):

---

1 "Reims marked the true acceptance of the aeroplane as a practical vehicle and as such was a major milestone in the world's history", from *The Impact of Air Power on the British People and Their Government 1909–14*, p89

*Above left:* Hubert Latham
*Above right:* Louis Paulhan
*(Philip Jarrett Collection)*

"Having passed the following tests, except those taken abroad under the rules of the Aéro Club de France, three separate flights must be made, each of three miles around a circular course without coming to the ground. These flights need not necessarily be made on the same day. On the completion of each flight the engine must be stopped in the air, and a landing effected within 150 yards of a given spot previously designated by the candidate to the official observers."[2]

This was by no means as easy as it perhaps sounds. At a distance of more than a century it is difficult for us now imagine what the novel experience of flying in a fairly primitive early aeroplane would have felt like. Captain Frederick Sykes was 32 years old in 1910. Thirty years later he described learning to fly as follows:

"Few people nowadays are able to visualize the difficulties and dangers of learning to fly in 1910. Five o'clock in the morning is not a time when one feels at one's best, and there were endless delays and false starts, while one hung about in the cold waiting for one's turn to come. There was an uncanny tension about trying to master in an unstable element the constant co-ordination of the movements of hand and foot, to keep the balance of the machine, and to develop this into subconscious action. There was something particularly unpleasant, too, in the effect of down currents, like sudden 'gaps in space'.

Dual control was not practicable; flying was in the experimental stage, it was impossible to predict how the frail and flimsy structure would behave in the air. Everything was 'by guess and by God' and we regarded ourselves as lucky if we landed without breaking something. It was a general rule for a pupil first to taxi about the aerodrome, then after he had got control of his machine on the ground to fly 'straights' down the field at a few feet from the surface. After this came the exciting moment of the first circuit.

2 *History of British Aviation*, p351

Major Frederick Sykes RFC with Queen Mary in 1913. The aeroplane is a Sopwith D.1. *(Author's Collection)*

Flying has always had a fascination for me, and I shall never forget the first occasion when I felt myself well above the ground, with the earth stretching away in all directions, I remember that during my first circuit I found myself outside the aerodrome with a man looking up at me from a field about two hundred feet below through the open space between my knees, and I was very uncertain whether I should be able to edge my plane round and return towards the friendly hangars."[3]

In those early days it was often contended that the skills required to handle a horse could be transferred to flying an aeroplane. The author, from his own experience as a competitive rider, would agree. Soft, responsive hands, sensitivity, anticipation, relaxed concentration and conquering the natural fear of a machine or beast with the latent potential to kill or seriously injure the pilot or rider are all important, along with the necessity of constant practice. It is significant that poor pilots were often referred to as ham-fisted. The other riding aids of voice, seat and legs on the girth are not quite so useful, though once again early fliers paid great reliance on flying by the seat of their pants, which clearly harks back to equestrian skills. Both the pilot and the rider must avoid over-confidence, the belief that you know it all and the failure to accept that if you do not treat the horse or machine with respect it will bite you in the bottom.

Nor should the difficulties of maintaining the machinery be forgotten, as the respected Irish journal, *The Motor News* noted:

3 *From Many Angles*, p89–90. Air Vice Marshal Sir Frederick Sykes (1877–1954) had a very distinguished career as a military officer, statesman and politician, serving as Chief of the Air Staff in 1918–19, as Controller of Civil Aviation, twice as a Member of Parliament and as Governor of Bombay.

"Sundry mechanics dance attention on that spoilt child of aviation – the Gnome engine. There is no doubt that this motor requires no end of attention in order to keep it in good order. It is the practice with this engine to remove all the cylinders and valves after every extended flight, and to give the whole outfit a thorough cleaning. For this, aviators are indebted to the use of castor oil, and inlet valves in the piston heads. The oil is flung through these valves by centrifugal force, and then finds its way out of the exhaust valves, to be finally deposited upon the front of the fuselage, the pilot, and the wings. This is the price one pays for a good aeronautical engine."[4]

## Ireland

In the first decade of the twentieth century Ireland was peaceful and relatively prosperous on the surface, with a population of more than 4 million, however, both nationalism and socialism were rising forces throughout the country, challenging the old order. The capital city, Dublin, was marked by extremes of poverty and wealth, reflected in its imposing Georgian architecture and squalid slums. It had some successful industries such as the Guinness brewery and Jacob's biscuits but could not compare with the advances made in the north. Belfast was enjoying the greatest boom in its history with economic success based on its industrial growth – shipbuilding, engineering, rope-making, distilling, tobacco and linen mills, making it one of the great industrial cities of the British Empire, though it too suffered from social problems. Elsewhere on the island prosperity, or the lack of it, was founded on trade, agriculture or land ownership. Following the land reform legislation of the nineteenth century and Wyndham's Act of 1903, by 1908 some 46% of Irish farmers had become owner-occupiers. Rural poverty was a major social ill, particularly in the west of the country, contrasting with the country estates of rich landowners.

One of the major engines of social change had been the development of a large railway network, linking small towns and providing a degree of mobility which had not existed before. Over 3500 miles of track were laid and it was said that at the height of its growth there was not a town in Ireland more than 10 miles from a railway station. Another facet of modern technology was in a much earlier stage of use, the motor car, though the Irish Automobile Club had been founded in January 1901, "to give a focus to those adventurous souls who had embraced the new automobilism," when it, "was still an adventure."[5] It has been asserted that, "Edwardians saw the motor grow in those halcyon days from a mechanical invention not without a savour of ridicule to a fact of transportation which was clearly marked to oust the horse."[6]

By 1910 this was indeed the case in Ireland with motor transport being used more and more for practical purposes rather than as just another sporting pastime for the wealthy. From the start of the decade when there were no more than 40 motor cars in the whole of

---

4  *The Motor News*, 14 September 1912
5  *Early Aviation in Ireland* by Bob Montgomery, p14
6  *The Fellowship of the Air*, p25

Ireland, adventurous motorists travelled all over the country allowing people to see cars for the first time. Indeed as early as 1901 the Irish Automobile Club (later the RIAC) organized a 1,000 mile tour travelling from Dublin through Waterford, Cork, Kerry, Clare, Galway, Connemara, Mayo, Sligo, Fermanagh, Monaghan, Cavan, Meath and back to Dublin. Irish roads were, however, very poor. They had no hard surface and in dry weather clouds of choking dust arose with the passage of a vehicle while in wet weather the road turned into a muddy quagmire. It is worth noting that the man who brought the first car into Ireland, John Brown of Dunmurry, Belfast, next founded the Irish Roads Improvement Association. Steam Rollers were very rare and for most of the 1900s there were only two in Ireland. One commercial organisation found it worthwhile to issue a map of steam-rolled roads in Ireland. It was only after the Great War that significant improvements to Irish roads were made.[7]

Ireland was by no means immune from the growing European interest in aviation. In the autumn of 1909 the *King's County Chronicle* reported as follows, "Mr Michael Carroll, cycle mechanic, conducted experiments in aviation in the hills adjoining Birr reservoir. An apparatus constructed from calico and bamboo made one or two fitful attempts to ascend. The incredulous may laugh at his efforts but it should not be forgotten that every great invention has its beginning in failure."[8] One week later it was noted that the Engineering and Scientific Association of Ireland (founded in Dublin in 1903) had been discussing aviation, "The opinion was expressed that flying through the air was not an accomplished fact, though eventually it would be, that flying was not of any practical use and that men now engaged in a series of experiments in aviation would not die in their beds."[9]

On 5 November 1909 the Aero Club of Ireland was founded in the Meeting Rooms of the Royal Irish Automobile Club in Dawson Street, Dublin, "for the encouragement and support

Members of the Irish Aero Club assemble in the garage of the Irish Automobile Club on 5 November 1909. *(Royal Irish Automobile Club)*

7  The author is grateful to Irish motoring historian, Bob Montgomery, for the information provided in this section.

8  *King's County Chronicle*, 20 October 1909

9  Ibid, 27 October 1909

John Moore-Brabazon and passenger. *(Author's Collection)*

of aerial navigation". Its members included such luminaries as Harry Ferguson, John Dunville, John Boyd Dunlop (1840–1921)[10] and John Moore-Brabazon[11] (who would become the holder of Aviator's Certificate No 1 issued by the Royal Aero Club on 8 March 1910). The Club's aim was to hold aerial meetings and competitions and to bring eminent airmen to Ireland to demonstrate their machines and their own flying skills. The annual subscription was agreed at one guinea.

John Moore-Brabazon commences the first all-British circular flight of one mile at Shellbeach in a Short biplane on 30 October 1909. *(Author's Collection)*

The claim mentioned above that Brabazon was the first Englishman to fly in England caused some debate in the letter pages of *Flight* magazine, which itself had appeared for the first time in January 1909. One reader, Maurice J Dodd, from Castlerea in Co Roscommon was unimpressed, writing, "You refer to Mr Moore-Brabazon as the first Englishman to fly in a heavier-than-air machine. Over here

---

10  John Boyd Dunlop was one of the founders of the rubber company that bore his name, Dunlop Pneumatic Tyre Company. He was born on a farm in Dreghorn, North Ayrshire, and studied to be a veterinary surgeon at the University of Edinburgh, moving to Downpatrick, Co Down in 1867. There established Downe Veterinary Clinic with his brother James, before moving to a practice in Belfast. In 1887, he developed the first practical pneumatic or inflatable tyre.

11  *The Fellowship of the Air,* p43. The author describes Brabazon thus, "an extremely handsome young man; with full lips, calm and discerning eyes, and dark hair brushed in a sweep off a wide forehead. Unlike most of his fellow aeronauts, he had no drooping moustache, and that omission accentuates the firm jaw and chin of this young man."

we call him an Irishman."[12] Another, signing himself 'Irishman', added, "Is it not a fact that Mr JTC Moore-Brabazon is an Irishman, and if this is the case why not state it, at least in as a prominent a place as the notice about him in your issue of November 6th, 1909?"[13] The Editor, Stanley Spooner (1856–1940), "a methodical, plodding, cheeseparing craftsman in ink"[14] responded, "Mr Moore-Brabazon's Irish descent is so well-known that that must be our excuse for the obvious omission of the statement from our 'history' last week. We can assure our correspondent, who, by the way, is a much-esteemed motorist, that there was no intention on our part of doing an injustice to Ireland."[15] Brabazon was born in London but was the son of Lieutenant Colonel Moore-Brabazon of Tara Hill, Co Meath and was descended from the 7th Earl of Meath, so can certainly be claimed as an Anglo-Irishman.

Charles Rolls at the controls of his Wright biplane. *(Author's Collection)*

When asked by the *Pall Mall Gazette* in February 1909 what are the necessary qualifications for flying he replied, "Plenty of spare time and a good deal of spare cash."

He was deeply upset by the death of his friend, Charles Rolls (1877–1910), who, on 12 July 1910 at Bournemouth, was the first Briton to be killed in a flying accident and withdrew from flying himself, though he also said that this decision was based on the changing nature of aviation with the gentleman amateur being superceded by the professional manufacturer.

The intention of this account is to describe and examine the key events in the field of aviation in Ireland during the bare five years between Harry Ferguson's first flight and the outbreak of the Great War; to describe the people, the aircraft and the places; to make as much use of contemporary sources as possible, to quote extensively from these and so see through the eyes of those who witnessed these exciting times.

---

12  *Flight,* 13 November 1909
13  Ibid
14  *The Fellowship of the Air,* p66
15  *Flight,* 13 November 1909

Chapter 1
# Pioneers

## Harry Ferguson

Iᴛ ɪs ɢᴇɴᴇʀᴀʟʟʏ ᴀᴄᴄᴇᴘᴛᴇᴅ that on 31 December 1909, Harry Ferguson (1884–1960), who came from farming stock in Growell, a village near Dromore in Co Down, made the first aeroplane flight in Ireland at Large Park, Hillsborough, Co Down, in a monoplane of his own design, powered by an eight-cylinder, 35 hp (26 kW), air-cooled JAP engine (from the manufacturers, JA Prestwich of London). He started out as an apprentice in 1902 in Belfast and then worked for his brother Joe's firm, JB Ferguson & Co, as a motorcycle and automobile mechanic. By 1909 this skilled natural engineer was the Works Manager and a Director of the company, which had been established in Belfast in 1903, firstly at 41 Little Donegall Street and

The Ferguson Mk 1 at JB Ferguson & Co, Chichester Street, Belfast in October 1909.
*(via Ernie Cromie)*

then, in 1909, moved to larger premises in Chichester Street. Harry became convinced that designing, building and flying an aeroplane would be great publicity for the business. The press reported his flight with a large headline and photographs:

HISTORIC EVENT AT HILLSBOROUGH – FIRST FLIGHT ACCOMPLISHED
"The first successful flight of an Irish built and owned aeroplane has been accomplished. It is, in fact, the first flight of an aeroplane in this country. The event in future years, when the development of aeroplaning has become an accomplished fact, will be recorded as of era-dating importance. The recent discussions that have taken place in respect of the early stages of the evolution of the Dunlop tyre show how necessary it is that in the interests of historical accuracy this event should be properly noticed, for the history of aeroplaning in this country will date from December 3lst, 1909 – a date that should be easily remembered.

It was only a few days subsequent to the flying week at Blackpool [October 1909], which followed that at Rheims [August 1909] that Mr Harry G Ferguson, one of the firm of JB Ferguson, Ltd, Belfast, actually began the construction of his aeroplane.

Prior to that, together with Mr James M'Kee, he had carefully considered the problem of aeronautics as applied to aeroplaning, and a set of plans for the construction of a. machine involving some novel features had been carefully thought out and drafted. Having had the opportunity of examining the best machines in the world, both at Rheims and at Blackpool, he was satisfied that he was upon absolutely right lines, and the work of construction was at once commenced. Every part of the machine except the engine and propeller is practically the work of Mr Ferguson's own hands, and every scrap of it was constructed, in the firm's workshops under his own personal supervision. The engine is an eight-cylinder JAP air-cooled, which, it is obvious, gives more than ample power for the purpose of the most ambitious flight, and Mr Ferguson, it may be added, has very considerable ambitions in this direction. To Blériot of France has fallen the honour of being the first to fly the English Channel. It will not come as any surprise should Mr Ferguson be the first to fly the Irish Channel – at all events, it is certain that he will make such an attempt in the near future, weather permitting.

It is exactly three weeks ago that Mr Ferguson had his aeroplane removed to the Old Park at Hillsborough, Co Down, for the purpose of making initial experiments. The weather since then has been most unsuitable, high winds, snowstorms, violent rains, and dense fogs having at one period or another prevailed, and prevented the aerial navigator from conducting his trials. Shortly before Christmas an opportunity was given to make an experiment, but it was found that the propeller fitted was not sufficient to permit of anything in the form of a flight proper, and Mr Ferguson had to content himself with slight rises a short distance from the ground, which were carried out in the presence of a number of visitors.

A new propeller, supplied by Cochrane[1], arrived during the week, and was fitted on Thursday afternoon, and everything being in readiness, Mr Ferguson for the

Harry Ferguson at Large Park Hillsborough in December 1909. *(Author's Collection)*

1  The Cochrane Propeller Co, London

first time made a trial under conditions favourable in all respects except those of weather yesterday, the last day of the year, for he had set his heart upon being able to say that the first flight in Ireland had been made in 1909. The wind when he made the attempt was blowing at a rate of 25 miles per hour, which at periods was considerably exceeded in violent gusts of almost cyclonic force. Although friends were apprehensive of trials under such circumstances, Mr Ferguson would not be dissuaded from his purpose, and having had the machine carefully looked over, the engine was set going. The exhaust is a perfectly free one, and without a silencer of any kind, so that the roar of the eight cylinders, was like the sound of a Gatling gun in action.

Harry Ferguson in the Mk1b at Masserene Park, Antrim in February 1910. *(Author's Collection)*

The machine was set against the wind, and all force being developed, the splendid pull of the new propeller swept the big aeroplane along as Mr Ferguson advanced the lever. Presently at the movement of the pedal, the aeroplane rose into the air at a height, of from nine to twelve feet, amidst the hearty cheers of the onlookers. The poise of the machine was perfect, and Mr Ferguson made a splendid flight of about 130 yards. Although fierce gusts of wind made the machine wobble a little twice, the navigator steadied her by bringing her head to the wind. Then he brought the machine to earth safely after having accomplished probably the most successful initial flight that has ever been attempted upon an aeroplane. Mr Ferguson is to be congratulated upon the success which has so far attended his efforts in aeronautics, and his future achievements will be awaited with eager interest."[2]

Unfortunately, the undulating and hilly terrain at Hillsborough wasn't particularly suitable for flying so Harry continued his experiments in Masserene Park at Antrim. By April 1910, he had sufficient confidence in his personal and the machine's capability that he gave short flights to a couple of Boy Scouts who were encamped nearby, Patrol Leader Joseph L Tegart, Wolf Patrol, and Scout FR Allen of the 15th Belfast Troop. It is likely that these flights were no more than short hops according to Ferguson's biographer, Michael Clarke.

From June onwards, further successful flights were made on the beach at Magilligan Strand, Co Londonderry, which proved to be an almost ideal venue, being a seven-mile stretch of sand. The *Ballymena Weekly Telegraph* described an eventful afternoon:

"The news of his arrival had evidently been transmitted over a wide area, and on Sunday big crowds travelled to the strand in expectation of witnessing a flight. It is estimated that about 2000 persons were present, including some hundreds of the Hampshire Regiment at present in the neighbouring military camp.

2 *Belfast Evening Telegraph*, 1 January 1910

Harry Ferguson flying the Mk 1e at Magilligan in the later summer of 1910. *(Author's Collection)*

About six o'clock pm Mr Ferguson ordered his 'plane to be drawn down to the west strand, to the delight of the multitude. Seating himself in the craft, he started the engine, which drives the 7 ft propeller at a speed of 1500 revolutions per minute, and dashed along the strand, rising with a bold sweep to an altitude of about 35 ft. Pursuing a steady course above the strand at this height for three-quarters of a mile, the aviator turned his 'plane towards Lough Foyle and soared above the water for half a mile. On the return journey the wind made the craft rock violently, causing the monoplanist to bring down the machine prematurely into five feet of water. No sooner was the descent made than Mr Ferguson switched on his engine, and splashing along the water, the lower part of the 'plane submerged and the propeller deluging him with spray he rose clear of the tide midst the applause of the spectators, and regained the beach. Afterwards he made some elevating trials and finished with a half-mile flight, arriving at his starting point amid cheers."[3]

A few days later he took to the air again:

"Towards evening on Thursday the stiff breeze had moderated somewhat, and the aviator decided to have another flight prior to going to County Down. A very tricky wind was blowing at 7.30 o'clock when the 'plane was wheeled down be strand, and the spectators sought points of vantage. Mr Ferguson first made a series of short flights, running before the wind across the wide, firm strand, and afterwards wheeling westwards, he made a rapid run until almost out of sight, the roar of the engine being, reduced to a faint hum in the distance. Swinging towards the Lough, he turned on his homeward journey, and skirting the water, he went along the beach for a short distance at a speed of 30 miles an hour, and rose most gracefully to a height of thirty feet, and soared steadily for almost a mile, the poise of the frail craft being perfect, before he alighted. It was a very pretty sight. On Friday the monoplane was dismantled, prior to conveyance to Newcastle, County Down, after which he will return at an early date to Magilligan Point for further experiment. With the improvements he has effected he is now in possession of a very reliable and steady aeroplane."[4]

---

3  *Ballymena Weekly Telegraph*, 23 July 1910
4  Ibid

In July he was persuaded by the offer of a prize of £100 to fly his aircraft for a distance of two miles at Newcastle, Co Down. His initial attempts were unsuccessful, one being rudely terminated when he sustained damage to a wheel and propeller on landing. *The Times* noted:

> "Mr Harry Ferguson made a second attempt on Saturday [23rd July] to fulfil his contract with the Newcastle Co Down Sports Committee to fly a distance of two miles on the foreshore. After making five ascents the machine came suddenly to the ground, breaking the propeller and one of the wheels. The machine was at once repaired but after a short flight there was another accident which broke a wheel, and further attempts were abandoned."[5]

*Above left:* Harry Ferguson at Newcastle in July 1910. *(Ernie Cromie Collection)*

*Above right:* Harry Ferguson in July 1910 at Donard Park, Newcastle with the Mk 1d. *(Author's Collection)*

Undeterred, by 8 August 1910 he was back at Newcastle where, with a repaired and overhauled aircraft, he flew well over two miles along the beach at a height of between 50 and 100 feet and won the prize. This, incidentally, was Ireland's first officially observed flight.

Later in August he made the first flight in Ireland to carry a passenger, a brave lady by the name of Miss Rita Marr.[6] Rita's father was Edward Marr who photographed the scene. He was the son of Lawrence Marr whose business, Lawrence Marr and Son Ltd, is still in operation as a building and civil engineering contractor in Liverpool. The *Belfast Evening Telegraph* reported:

---

5  *The Times*, 25 July 1910
6  Mary Margaret 'Rita' Marr (1888–1941) was born in Liverpool, her mother, Estelle, was from Castlebar in Co Mayo and her father, Edward, had family roots in Co Kildare. The *Liverpool Daily Post* of Thursday, 15 April 1915 noted as follows: "GARRY – MARR – April 14, at St Clare's, Sefton Park, Dr Michael Garry, of Triniderry, Ennis, Co Clare, eldest son of Patrick Garry, JP, to Rita, only daughter of Edward L Marr, of Grove House, Sefton Park Road, Liverpool." They subsequently had four children. They lived in Co Clare for ten years before returning to Lancashire.

## AVIATION IN CO DERRY – MR FERGUSON'S EXPERIMENTS – FLIGHT WITH LADY PASSENGER

"Mr Harry Ferguson, the young Belfast aviator, returned to Magilligan Point last week after his stubborn and triumphant battle with the elements at Newcastle (Co Down), and resumed his experiments in aviation on Monday, after effecting a thorough overhaul and readjustment of his Belfast-built monoplane. In the afternoon the plane was taken down to the beach, where, in presence of numerous spectators, Mr Ferguson made a series of flights, attaining a height of from 30 to 50 feet. The little aircraft behaved splendidly, the pilot apparently having perfect control of it, notwithstanding the atmospheric influences he had to contend with. The aviator also performed a series of aerial evolutions, which thrilled the spectators, above whom he executed a number of encircling movements with singular grace. Afterwards Mr Ferguson achieved the distinction of being the first aviator in Ireland to perform a flight with a lady passenger. Miss Rita Marr, of Liverpool, a visitor at Magilligan

Point, who was an interested spectator of Mr Ferguson's work in mid-air, pluckily undertook to accompany him in a flight, and, amidst great applause, took her seat with him. The 35-hp, eight-cylindered engine was set in motion, and the pilot and passenger sped along the strand and rose into the air, travelling a considerable distance, to the delight of the spectators, who accorded the couple an ovation when they returned,

Sitting among the dunes at Magilligan, Rita Marr is on the left and Harry Ferguson reclines to her left. *(Edward Marr)*

A press cutting (thought to be from a local newspaper in Co Clare during the First World War) featuring Rita Marr. *(via Tammy Travers)*

Harry Ferguson at Magilligan in August 1910. *(Edward Marr)*

and Miss Marr was congratulated on being the first lady passenger on a monoplane in this country."[7]

In October of that year he had a setback at Magilligan with a crash that left his machine a wreck. He flew again in 1911, undertaking to appear at the North Down Agricultural Society Show at Newtownards on 15 June. While practising a few days earlier he had to make a forced landing on the sands. *Flight* magazine noted:

"Since the accident to his machine at Magilligan last year Mr Harry Ferguson has constructed a new monoplane, and having arranged to give a demonstration at Newtownards on Thursday of last week be had the machine towed down to that place by motor from Belfast on Monday. As soon as the machine reached the beach Mr Ferguson fitted the wings to it and, starting the engine, was off the ground for his first flight in 50 yards. This little essay was entirely unpremeditated as the wind was blowing a good half gale, and Mr Ferguson had no intention of flying under the circumstances. The lift, however, was so great that a strong gust got its work in, and, owing to the nature of the ground, the wind velocity rose as the machine rose, and of course kept it going on up. Mr Ferguson tried to land nearly a dozen times, and every time as he dropped and got into the slower moving air below, the machine dived, and he had to go right up again to save from damage. Mr Ferguson had a very exciting time, but even then he would have landed perfectly after his mile flight, but for a crowd of people getting in the way. In order to avoid them, be had actually to dive suddenly from a height of 20 ft, and it was very fortunate that be escaped personal injury. The only damage done to the machine consisted of a few broken wires, a damaged skid, and a smashed propeller. It speaks well for the design and construction of the machine, however, that it should fly so well under such conditions, and it should give a good account of itself in the hands of Mr Ferguson during this summer season."[8]

The aeroplane was taken to James Miskelly's farm nearby – close to the site of what would become Ards Airfield. The undercarriage was repaired and a new propeller was fitted. Ferguson resumed flying and took up a passenger on two flights. Sadly he came to grief again with the result that only the wrecked aeroplane could be displayed at the show as a sorry looking static exhibit. *Flight* magazine again:

MR FERGUSON HAS A SMASH
"Ill luck, however, dogged this plucky young Irish aviator on Wednesday of last week, and as a result, his machine is completely wrecked. After making one or two good trials over the ground at Newtownards by himself he made two with passengers,

7  *Belfast Evening Telegraph*, 24 August 1910
8  *Flight,* 24 June 1911

Harry Ferguson poses
with Sam Turkington,
Miskelly's Farm near
Ards, October 1911.
*(Bombardier Belfast)*

including one weighing 13 stone. The last flight was also with a passenger, and after he had been carried for about a mile Mr Ferguson landed in good style from a height of 25 ft. Just as he landed and switched off the engine, however, the front wheel stuck in a small mud bank, causing the chassis to collapse and wrecking the machine. Unfortunately the passenger, who was one of Mr Ferguson's mechanics, was rather badly hurt, but he is making good progress and hopes to be all right in about a fortnight."[9]

The aftermath of Harry
Ferguson's crash at
Newtownards in 1911.
*(Author's Collection)*

He returned to Newtownards for the same purpose in October and was more successful but his time as a pioneer aviator was almost at an end. Nevertheless, Ferguson produced eight variants of his aircraft, including the prototype but of course he became more famous for his invention of the Three-Point Linkage and its role in the development of the modern agricultural tractor. A full-size replica of the Ferguson monoplane was constructed many years later by another renowned Irish airman, Captain Jack Kelly-Rogers (1905–1981)[10]. For some years it made a splendid sight, suspended above the concourse of Belfast International Airport at Aldergrove.

---

9 Ibid

10 John Cecil Kelly-Rogers was born in Dún Laoghaire. He flew with the RAF, Imperial Airways and BOAC, gaining fame as a flying boat pilot, piloting Winston Churchill to several wartime meetings. Many years later, as a senior manager with Aer Lingus, Captain Kelly-Rogers loved to recall his wartime experiences with the great Prime Minister – to such an extent that it was rumoured that Sir Winston was writing a new book, entitled 'I flew with Kelly-Rogers'.

A replica of the Ferguson Flyer used to hang from the ceiling at Belfast International Airport. *(Author's Collection)*

## Lilian Bland

Lilian Bland (1878–1971) also designed and flew her own aircraft, the first biplane constructed in Ireland and the first aeroplane to be designed, built and tested by a woman anywhere in the world. While she was born in Kent on 28 September 1878, her family had deep roots in Ireland, Belfast and Whiteabbey. There had been Blands in Ireland since at least 1670. Her grandfather, the Reverend Robert Wintringham Bland MA, JP (1794–1880) who was born at Blandsfort in Queen's County and later studied at Trinity College, Dublin, had been the Perpetual Curate of Upper Falls at St George's Church in Belfast between 1825 and 1836, the oldest Anglian place of worship in the city. From 1845 to 1849 he was the District Curate of St John's Parish Church at Whitehouse, a few miles from the city, in Co Antrim on the north shore of Belfast Lough. With his wife, Alicia, who was from Dungannon, he raised a family of six children in Whiteabbey, a mile or so along the coast from Whitehouse. His eldest son, John Humphrey Bland (1828–1919) became an artist. Between 1848 and 1861, having gained a BA at Trinity, he studied art in Paris, exhibiting his work at the Royal Academy in London and the Belfast Art Society. In 1867 he married Emily Charlotte Madden; they had three children, of whom Lilian was the youngest. When his wife became ill in 1900, John Humphrey brought his family back to Ireland where he set up home at Tobarcorran House in the village of Carnmoney with his sister, Mrs Sarah Smythe (1832–1918)[11].

Lilian had already made a name for herself as a journalist for both local Irish papers

---

11  The widow of the distinguished, Carnmoney-born soldier, General WJ Smythe (1816–1887)

*Above:* A portrait photograph of Lilian taken in 1907. *(Ulster Aviation Society)*

*Above right:* Lilian riding in Carnmoney. *(via Mrs Nora Schwab)*

and London magazines and as an acclaimed press photographer. She further astonished her contemporaries in Carnmoney and scandalized her aunt, by wearing riding breeches, smoking cigarettes in public, tinkering with motor car engines and riding astride rather than side-saddle. She was also one of the first ladies in Ireland to apply for a jockey's licence. She rode for a training stables, riding exercises, trial gallops, schooling and breaking-in hunters and qualifying thoroughbreds for point-to-point races. She hunted in Antrim, Down, King's County (now Co Offaly), Queen's County (now Co Laois), Kilkenny and Tipperary in Ireland and with the Pytchley, Atherstone, North Warwick and Warwickshire Hunts in England.[12] Moreover, she was a crack shot and was not averse to lying in wait for poachers, before sending them and their lurchers packing with a well-aimed burst of shotgun pellets.

All of these characteristics were sufficient to make her stand out anywhere in the British Isles during the Edwardian period and rather more so in Presbyterian Ulster. She had become interested in aviation through her hobby of photographing bird life; in particular she had become fascinated by the seagulls wheeling in the skies over the west coast of Scotland while she was staying with friends at Roshven near Kinlochmoidart on the west coast of Scotland in the summer of 1908. She subsequently wrote about this:

> "I was off to the Highlands to photograph sea birds, with a large trunkful of negatives and Lumiere[13] colour plates. I would lie for hours studying the great black backed gulls soaring, using their tails as balancing rudders to the shifting breeze – how lovely it would be to fly."[14]

12  *The Mercury*, Hobart, Tasmania 7 January 1907.
13  The *Focal Press Encyclopaedia* describes the first practical system of colour photography. It was named Autochrome by its inventors August and Louis Lumiere in 1903. Manufacture began in Lyons in 1907. "It was always about 50 times less sensitive than contemporary black-and-white materials. In its grain pattern and its palette, Autochrome resembled French impressionist paintings with its lovely textures and pastel hues."
14  E-mail from the Reverend Edward Pratt to the author.

Later that year she exhibited, at the Royal Photographic Society's Annual Exhibition in London, a selection of twelve of the colour photographs which she had produced, which she believed were the first colour plates of live birds to be taken. When in the following year, Louis Blériot flew across the English Channel on July 25th, her Uncle Robert sent her a postcard of the Blériot XI monoplane[15] including a note of the machine's dimensions, her aviation ambitions were further kindled. She was an avid reader of *Flight* magazine, often sending letters to the editor and attended the Blackpool Aviation Meeting. *Flight's* editor, Stanley Spooner, commented on one missive as follows:

> "It is at all times a pleasure to us to receive such a thoroughly helpful letter, and the fact that it comes from a lady only enhances the interest which attaches to it, but shows how far-reaching is the fascination of flight. We expect much from Ireland in aviation, as in every other phase of daring sport, and we cordially wish success to our correspondent."[16]

The cover of the programme for Blackpool's Aviation Week in 1909. *(Blackpool International Airport)*

Lilian was highly observant and by no means uncritical; she was not over-awed by either the magnificent men or their flying machines. She made a careful inspection of the aircraft, measuring and recording their dimensions, examining their structures, method of construction and engines. Many years later the Department of Aeronautical Engineering at Queen's University, Belfast examined her notebooks and technical drawings and commented very favourably on her technical skills and grasp of the subject.

During the winter of 1909–10 Lilian designed and manufactured her aeroplane from spruce, ash, elm and bamboo, covered with unbleached calico, which she doped with a home-mixed concoction of gelatine and formalin, having previously built a model glider which she flew successfully. She decided to name her aeroplane the *Mayfly* on the eminently practical grounds that it "may fly or may not". The *Mayfly* was flown as a glider in the spring of 1910 on the slopes of Carnmoney Hill, with the assistance of her aunt's gardener's 'boy', Joe Blain (1878–1955) and, subsequently, four stalwart members of the Royal Irish Constabulary. The lifting qualities of the *Mayfly* were so good that the four constables were in danger of becoming test pilots, so they released their hold with great alacrity, leaving Joe Blain to cling on, turn the

Sam Girvan and Joe Blain with the *Mayfly* on Carnmoney Hill. *(JM Bruce GS Leslie Collection)*

---

15  Several of the early visitors to Ireland would use the Blériot XI. This neat tractor monoplane first flew in January 1909. The airframe was made from steel tube, ash and bamboo, which was partially covered by rubberised and waterproofed fabric.

16  *Flight*, 11 December 1909

glider out of wind and bring it back to earth. In July she caught the ferry to England and returned with an AVRO 20 hp (15 kW) engine and propeller. Two other passengers on the boat train asked the purpose of her baggage – "To make an aeroplane" she replied, "What is an aeroplane?" was the response. The engine was test run with the aid of a whiskey bottle filled with petrol and her aunt's ear trumpet. An engine mounting was added to the trailing edge of the lower wing, a canvas seat was furnished for the leading edge, a T-bar control yoke was fitted and a tricycle undercarriage was constructed. The *Mayfly* was configured as a pusher with the engine behind the pilot.

Lilian in flight in February 1911. *(Flight)*

The Avro 20 hp engine installed on the *Mayfly*. *(Flight)*

The small field at Carnmoney was judged to be inadequate for flight trials; instead Lord O'Neill's 800 acre park at Randalstown was made available. Small wheels were fitted to the skids, while the front and rear booms were removed, which enabled the *Mayfly* to be towed to its new location and then re-erected. The field also apparently was home to a bull, which as Lilian wrote to *Flight*, "If it gets annoyed and charges I shall have every inducement to fly!"[17] When the weather was suitable – calm with little or no wind – Joe and Lilian would cycle the twelve miles over to Randalstown. The first tentative hops were made in August 1910. At first the aviatrix could scarcely believe that she had left the ground until viewing the evidence – as the cessation and resumption of the wheel tracks denoted her flight path. The flights increased in length to nearly a quarter of a mile and the *Belfast Evening Telegraph* declared on 7 September[18],

FIRST IRISH BIPLANE TO FLY. CO ANTRIM LADY'S SUCCESSES IN AVIATION
"Miss Bland of Carnmoney, Co Antrim, who is the first lady to design and construct an aeroplane, has been making short flights with her machine near Randalstown. The biplane was first tested as a glider, and proved so successful that Miss Bland decided to fit it with a motor. Since the aeroplane has been on its flying ground

---

17   *Flight*, 16 July 1910
18   *Belfast Evening Telegraph*, 7 September 1910

*Lilian Bland at the controls of the Mayfly. (Flight)*

the weather has been most unfavourable but the machine at its first trial rose from the ground after a run of thirty feet and flew for some distance a few feet above the ground. The machine is built somewhat on the lines of a Curtiss biplane but has two elevators working separately or together in connection with the horizontal tailplanes. The machine carries over 2lb per square foot, and weighs, with the pilot, under 600lbs. The motor is a 20 hp Avro two-cylinder opposed type and has so far proved most satisfactory and reliable."

Further letters and photographs appeared at regular intervals in *Flight* culminating in a major three page article, written by Lilian herself, in the 17th December 1910 issue, which also included a plan scale drawing of the aeroplane and detailed sketches of technical details. She compared the skills required when flying an aeroplane with those which also came in handy when hunting on horseback.

"When the engine starts, the draught from the propeller lifts the tail and the tip of the skids off the ground, and the machine balances on the two wheels; the third wheel in front only comes into action over rough ground, and to prevent the machine from going on her nose; it answers the purpose admirably, as my practice ground is rough grass with ridge and furrow, which on hunting principles I take at a slant."[19]

19  *Flight*, 17 December 1910

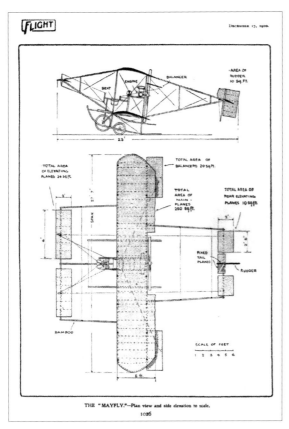

*Above:* A plan of the *Mayfly* from *Flight* magazine 1910. *(Flight)*

*Above right:* Lilian driving the Model T Ford purchased for her by her father. *(via Mrs Nora Schwab)*

In 1911 Lilian was bribed by the offer of a motor car from her elderly father to pursue less hazardous activities. She collected the car, a 20 hp (15 kW) Model T Ford, in Dublin and half-way back to Belfast took her first and only driving lesson. She then set up a sub-agency in Belfast selling Fords, which was announced in *Flight* and brought down further ire from her aunt, as being most unladylike. More shocks were to come as, in October Lilian married her cousin, Lieutenant Charles Loftus Bland (1881–1973). Charles had become a lumberjack in Canada and there Lilian would join him in April 1912 to carve out a new life in establishing a farm on 160 acres of land at Quatsino Sound, Vancouver Island in British Columbia. They had a daughter, Pat, who tragically died in 1929 at the age of 16, after contracting tetanus following an accident. Lilian returned to England alone in 1935, to live with her brother, Captain Robert Bland (1872–1942), at Penshurst in Kent. In 1965 she told the *New York Times*,

> "When I came back from Canada I became a gardener. I gambled my wages on the stock market and was very lucky. I made enough to come here [Sennen in Cornwall] ten years ago. I now spend my time painting, gardening and gambling a little."[20]

Lilian Bland died on 11 May 1971 at the age of 92 and is buried in the churchyard of the village of Sennen, near Land's End in Cornwall.

## Joseph Cordner

There is a view, particularly in the north-west, that the first Irishman to build and fly his own heavier-than-air craft was Joseph Cordner (1875–1960) of Derryinver, Co Armagh. His family was by no means well off, his father worked for one of the local landowners and Joe was entirely self-taught as regards design, engineering and mechanics. He had set up a

20  *New York Times*, 30 March 1965

bicycle shop with his twin brother in Lurgan and had moved to Londonderry in 1908. His exploits on the White Strand between Lisfannon and Buncrana in Co Donegal and at the Waterside, Londonderry, have been covered with a veil of obscurity. However recent research by Michael Clarke has been able to demonstrate that Cordner built and tested three monoplanes of his own design during the period 1908–1912. The monoplanes' wings were constructed to an unusual triangular lattice design with v-shaped ducts which were part of a patented control system, which Michael believes was questionable aerodynamically.[21] They were powered firstly by a 35 hp (26 kW) JAP engine and then by a 50 hp (37 kW) Anzani. His series of experiments terminated following an accident in 1912 at Eglinton when the Cordner Special broke free from its tethers when the engine was being run up and crashed, pilotless into a tree. No firm date can be established nor is there evidence to show that the flights were any more than short hops though it is also contended that two local boys were taken up as passengers on separate occasions. There is evidence that he tried to bring his work to public attention and to raise some funding. The *Donegal News* carried this advert in 1912:

Joe Cordner.
*(via Terry Mace)*

"Come and see Cordner's patent monoplane at Bond's Hotel Yard, Carlisle Road for two weeks from 17th June. The World's Greatest Patent Aeroplane designed and

---

21  Conversation with the author

Joe Cordner on the foreshore at Lisfannon near Buncrana. *(Michael Clarke Collection)*

constructed by Joseph Cordner, Royal Cycle Works, 5 John Street, Derry. It is fitted with an eight-cylinder 40 hp engine. The Aeroplane is the only one of its type in the world. Adults 1/-, Children 3d."[22]

The only one of the three Ulster pioneers to obtain a Royal Aero Club 'ticket' and so become a fully licenced pilot was Joe Cordner at the Hall School of Flying, Hendon in 1916 (No 3545 on 6 September). Joseph Cordner returned home in May 1919, with fellow Ulster airman, Geoffrey Smiles[23] (1889–1922) (RAeC Certificate No 783, 14 May 1914). He had also been an instructor at the Hall Flying School.

They flew a war surplus Avro 504 from London to North Antrim, crossing over from Turnberry on the Ayrshire coast, to give a series of pleasure flights around Coleraine and Ballycastle, as well as over Ballymoney, the Giant's Causeway and Bushmills. A demonstration was made of Joe Cordner's aerial bag for carrying and distributing mails, papers and parcels, when packets containing a special edition of the *Northern Constitution* were delivered on a Friday evening by air to outlying villages in the region of Ballymoney. It was thereby claimed in the newspaper that it was the first in Ireland to be distributed by air. Smiles was the son of William Holmes Smiles (1846–1904) the Managing Director of the Belfast Rope Works, the largest in the world at that time, the brother of Sir Walter Smiles (1883–1953), who perished in the *Princess Victoria* disaster in 1953 and the grandson of Dr Samuel Smiles (1812–1904), the author of *Self-Help*[24]. One of their passengers contributed this anonymous article to the *Northern Constitution* describing the experience:

**AEROPLANE FLIGHTS FOR PASSENGERS.**

Messrs. GEOFFREY SMILES, a native of Belfast; and JOSEPH CORDNER, of Derry, both Licensed Pilots, who arrived at

**PORTRUSH**

BY AEROPLANE FROM LONDON,

ARE NOW TAKING PASSENGERS AT REASONABLE FARES FOR

**TRIPS IN THE AIR.**

To Book Flights write, phone, or wire to

"Pilots, Portrush Hotel."

An advert placed in the local press by Cordner and Smiles in 1919. *(Author's Collection)*

"You have asked me to give your readers an account of my initial trip through the air. Well, I cannot find words to describe all my sensations, but will try to tell you what I saw, and in a general way how I felt. On arriving in the field at Ballywillan I found the aeroplane, a great dark-coloured object, with wings outspread, waiting for me in charge of its two courteous attendants. The latter carefully inspected the mechanical parts of the plane, and then, turning to me with a smile, said 'Are you ready?' I was moderately ready. So I climbed into the little cockpit between the wings, and took some pains to see that the safety-belt was properly clinched up, feeling all the while that Columbus took a very small chance indeed when he sailed out into an unknown ocean in a real, floating, solid boat.

---

22 *Donegal News*, 22 June 1912

23 *Flight* of 26 January 1922 noted that he was, "an exceptionally skilful and daring pilot. As an instructor he was one of the best… understanding the individuality of each pupil and winning his absolute confidence."

24 One of the most popular books of the 19th century, published in 1859, it promoted thrift and claimed that poverty was largely the consequence of irresponsible habits.

A civil registered Avro
504. *(via Colin Cruddas)*

If you have noticed how a seagull on the strand runs along for a yard or two
before it takes to flight, you will have some idea of our start. The engine was turned
on, we ran down the field and quickly left terra firma. In a moment or two we were
passing over cottages and farmhouses, brown fields and green ones. The plane
swayed a little, as its nose was turned southwards, whereat feelings of alternate fear
and pleasure passed over me. My chief fear was that something might break, and
permit us to fall on the bosom of a hard, unfeeling earth with a sickening thud.

We rose gradually, and in a few minutes I noticed a short way ahead a cluster of
houses and shining roofs. This was Coleraine. The town looked as if it could be covered
by the hat I usually wear when I am in the lower world. Then I caught sight of the river
Bann glittering away to the south like a long piece of silk ribbon. The machine pitched
and swayed slightly as we made a wide semi-circle and turned towards the east. The
whirring propeller in front of me flung back solid masses of air. Just then I noticed that
the pilot was firmly gripping the 'joy stick'. Did the plane roll to the right? He shoved
the stick gently to the left, and back to an even keel it came. When its nose pointed too
abruptly to the heavens he shoved the stick forward. I saw that the pilot's feet rested on
another control, the rudder, which turned the plane's head right and left.

When over Coleraine I could see Portrush quite distinctly basking in the sunshine.
The plane was now roaring eastward at a considerable height, and the country below
was becoming less and less distinctly marked by hedges and roads. The land seemed
to be fading and contracting, slowly into a large-scale-map. A tiny steamship was far
below; behind it were two trails, one of white water and the other of black smoke.
Then there were green fields below again, and then dirty brown houses separated
into small groups. It took a mental argument for me to convince myself that what I
saw was Bushmills. I peered somewhat nervously over the side and realised that we
were sailing over the Causeway coast. The two hotels were like a child's toy houses.
Ballintoy next glided into view; a mere streak on the shore. Glancing backward,
Portrush appeared to be amazingly near, it seemed as if you could place one foot
there and the other in Ballintoy.

Rough country was now before us and the pilot found it wise to keep well towards the 'ceiling'. Presently we reached Ballycastle, over which we hung in space for a minute or two. The pilot pointed the machine a few degrees to the north, not running any risk, as I supposed, of crashing into Knocklayde, and in moment or two we were tearing homewards at full speed. Fields and farmhouses crept far below. I was now thinking of our landing place, remembering – what I had been told – that a plane will glide one mile for every thousand feet it ascends. The engine hummed on and on and as we neared Portrush the plane began to drop. Occasionally cars and horses came into view on the roads. The nose of the machine dipped the more, and it seemed as if we were going to crash into the Metropole Hotel. Next we came in sight of the long green field from which we started. The motor continued to roar, but was then shut off, and we glided towards the field. Something hit the machine a jarring blow – another jolt – then a succession of jolts. Then I realised we were bumping along solid ground. 'Here ends the first trip,' was the pilot's remark in the unearthly stillness that followed the stopping of the motor."[25]

On 14 June 1919 the *Donegal News* reported that Messrs Cordner and Smiles had arrived in Co Antrim for the purpose of giving pleasure flights and had been provided with a suitable field near Portrush. Cordner was less than pleased with the authorities in Derry City, who had offered to rent him a field at £100 per week, despite the fact that his Motor & Cycle Works was based in the city. Moreover it noted that the public static exhibition of his machine (which had cost him £600 to construct) in 1912, raised just 2/9 in gate receipts.[26]

## Frank Aldritt

It has always seemed odd to this author that the three Irish pioneers to construct and fly their own aeroplanes were all from northern counties. However honourable mention should be made of Professor George Francis Fitzgerald (1851–1901) FRS of Trinity College, Dublin, who conducted experiments in 1895 in the College grounds with a Lilienthal No 11 glider, which he had purchased in kit form for £25 by mail order from Otto Lilienthal[27] himself. In King's County (now Co Offaly) in about 1896 the Honourable Sir Charles Algernon Parsons (1854–1931), the inventor of the compound steam turbine, built a model flying machine powered by steam but there is no evidence of it having flown successfully.

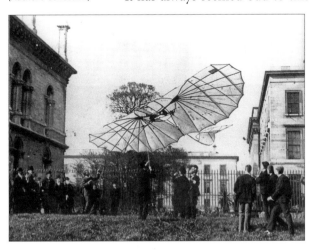

Professor Fitzgerald and his glider at Trinity College, Dublin. *(Author's Collection)*

25 *Northern Constitution,* May 1912
26 *Donegal News,* 14 June 1919
27 Otto Lilienthal (1848–96) was the first to study gliding flight scientifically, making over 2000 flights, before suffering serious injuries in an accident on 9 August 1896, from which he did not recover. The Wright brothers paid tribute to his work which was of great value to those who followed him.

The workshop at F Aldritt and Sons – the remains of the aeroplane can just be seen perched in the rafters. *(via Teddy Fennelly)*

The only example of an attempt at powered flight which I have been unable to uncover outside the old province of Ulster was made by Louis and Frank Aldritt of Maryborough in Queen's County (now Portlaoise in Co Laois). Starting in about 1908, they began to experiment with the design and construction of a monoplane, similar to a Blériot, in the workshop of their motor engineering business. It was powered by a three-cylinder, in-line, water-cooled engine, cast in Dublin by Tonge and Taggart. There is a considerable degree of uncertainty surrounding the question of whether it achieved flight or not. However, the *King's County Chronicle* of 4 November 1909 contained the following item:

> "It will be of interest to note that during the last week two brothers, Louis and Frank Aldritt, engineers of Maryborough, Queen's County, have succeeded in the presence of some friends in covering a short distance in a small aeroplane. The brothers a year ago designed a motor car which is a triumph of mechanical skill. They possess a high degree of mechanical skill, and have refused offers from across the Channel owing to a love of their native town."[28]

They were assisted by William Rogers and John Conroy and also by an Irish airman of the future, James Fitzmaurice[29] (1898–1965), who was a schoolboy at the time and who witnessed the crash of an early design, piloted by Frank Aldritt. In 1912 an attempt at

---

28  Ibid, 4 November 1909
29  Commandant Fitzmaurice of the Irish Air Corps was a member of the crew of the *Bremen* which made the first successful trans-Atlantic flight from east to west on 12–13 April 1928.

flight was made in a field that belonged to the parish priest and is now Christian Brothers School sports field. The Aldritts' biggest problem with their aircraft was in the design of an engine of sufficient power for sustained flight. In 1914 with a redesigned engine, the plane was conveyed by road to the Great Heath of Maryborough, where it took off successfully, became airborne and flew for several hundred yards before coming in to land once more.[30]

It was then stored up in the rafters of Aldritt's workshop on the corner of Railway Street and Tower Hill, where, for many years, "its visible propeller fired the imaginations of young

lads coming from the nearby Christian Brothers school".[31] An alternative account states that the engine had been test run and all the major parts had been constructed but sadly Aldritt died in 1913 before a trial flight could be made. A reference to this may be found in a letter written to *Flight* magazine by Graham Skillen in July 1967,[32] in which he stated that parts of the machine were still stored in the town. The Irish-built engine was broken up for scrap. Some of the airframe is now preserved in the Filching Manor Museum, Polegate, Sussex. Joe Rogers has visited the museum and adds:

Joe Rogers examines what remains of Frank Aldritt's aeroplane at Filching Manor Museum, Sussex.
(*Joe Rogers*)

"What a thrill it was for me to see the massive wings with the two main spars in each wing consisting of rather large round bamboo poles to which a total of 15 cross-members or ribs of a lightweight timber are attached – the canvas covering having long since gone. The fuselage too, minus its outer covering of course, is in remarkably good condition, complete with tail assembly, cockpit, seat, rudder bar and pedals. The complete aircraft including both large wings and fuselage is well preserved after 100 years and would be easy to restore to its original condition."[33]

## Arthur V Blake

Late in 1909 a report and accompanying photograph appeared in the *Belfast Evening Telegraph* of a monoplane under construction by Arthur V Blake, who owned a commercial garage for marine and general motor engineering, situated at Magheramorne, a small village on the lough shore, five miles (8km) south of Larne.[34] There is no evidence to show that this machine was either completed or flown.

Arthur Blake at Magheramorne in 1909.
(*Author's Collection*)

30  E-mail from Joe Rogers to the author
31  Ibid
32  *Flight,* 20 July 1967
33  E-mail from Joe Rogers to the author
34  *Belfast Evening Telegraph*, 20 December 1909

# Edward Arthur Geoghegan

In the issue of *Flight* magazine published on 3 September 1910,[35] reference was made to a list of Aeronautical Patents Published which had been applied for in 1909 and 1910. No 11090 and No 11754 were in the names of Geoghegan and Moore-Irvine and both bore the title Apparatus for aerial navigation. Two weeks later an article appeared in the *Ballymena Observer* under the heading, 'A New Flying Machine. Belfast Engineer's Claims. An Epoch-Making Invention.' The full text of this piece is reproduced below:

"Up to now the public has heard little or nothing of Mr Edward Arthur Geoghegan, a Belfast engineer, but if his theories as to flight prove to be correct he will, declares a London correspondent, become one of the most famous men of the day. For four years he has spent his whole time and money upon inventions connected with the improvement of apparatus for aerial navigation, and now he has been granted two master patents in every manufacturing country in the world. A large working model of an entirely new type of flying machine has been demonstrated by him before a member of the of the Army Council, and before eminent scientists and engineers, and they all agree that if his inventions and theories can be applied to manlifting machines he will bring about revolutions in warfare and in the navigation of the air.

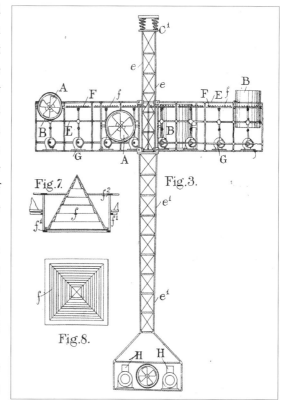

Part of Geoghegan's patent drawing of 11 May 1909. *(Author's Collection)*

The two great points about Mr Geoghegan's machine are that it is designed to rise direct into the air without any run over the ground and without any aid of planes or any form of balloon attachment. 'Hundreds of men have failed to gain direct lift by means of horizontal propellers because they put the whole weight of the machine against the screws directly they were started,' said Mr Geoghegan, in London to a Press representative. 'That did not give the propellers a chance. I have invented a means by which the propellers are not called upon to exert any lifting power until they have attained full speed. Then, rising to the summit of the machine and operating within a patent cylinder, they gradually lift the air car into space.'

'Three sets of smaller propellers, working vertically in large tubes, provide the driving and steering forces, while they can be so manipulated as to hold the air car stationary over any given spot. I could go up from a city street, circle the city, remain hovering over a selected building, and drop at an agreed minute in a confined area.

My air car will be safer than an aeroplane, because by the adoption of the gyroscopic principle it will always be in perfect balance, and in the event of the engine failing the machine would simply fall gradually, after the manner of a parachute.'

Mr Geoghegan is now engaged upon the construction of an aluminium and steel air car, designed to carry six men for a distance of 200 miles at a speed of 70 miles an hour. He hopes to be ready to take the air in November, and he trusts that if he gives successful flights the British and American Governments will offer him such support that he will have no need to take his invention to foreign countries."[36]

Thereafter Geoghegan is hard to trace, though an EA Geoghegan did file a number of US and UK patents in the 1920s concerned with the steam superheaters for marine boilers. Moreover a posting on Ancestry.co.uk states that Edward Arthur Geoghegan, an inventor from Banbridge, died in New York in 1936. It can certainly be said that he was ahead of the engineering technology of his time and from a drawing of his aerial navigation patent it may be surmised that his invention resembled a ducted fan.

## Isaac Bell

Remarkably (and owing to research carried out by Banbridge-born, Ernie Cromie) another native of that town filed several patents between 1912 and 1914. These concern: 'improvements in… flying machines' and describe at length and in detail various ideas, accompanied by well-executed drawings, including a form of flying machine with a system of flapping and non-flapping planes. It is highly unlikely that any would have been technically feasible, though it was reported some years ago in the *Banbridge Chronicle* that Bell, who was a local market gardener, attempted a trial flight at the Banbridge Farming Society's Annual Show. The machine failed to take off and shook itself to bits on the ground. Undaunted, Isaac Bell also bought an old railway turntable on which to mount his greenhouse, so that it always faced the sun, invented patent hedge clippers, a type of forge and an 'artificial sow', a rubber contraption which supplied warmed milk to piglets![37]

Copies of two letters written by Isaac Bell in December 1912 to Thomas Sinton of Tandragee have recently passed to the author. In these Bell is seeking financial support and writes:

"You have doubtless heard that for some time I have been working on a flying machine invention. For nearly three years I have given most of my time to the study and to experimenting on this subject, and am now in the possession of knowledge which when out into concrete form and practice, will master the problems of safe and economical flight, and revolutionize the world's methods of travelling. This may seem to you to be an impossibility, but it is nevertheless true, which I can prove and demonstrate to your satisfaction, or to the satisfaction of any reasonably and moderately intelligent mind."

36  *Ballymena Observer,* 16 September 1910
37  E-mail from Ernie Cromie to the author.

The purpose of developing a flying machine was, he stated, to spread the Christian gospel to all corners of the world. The second letter is much shorter than the first and expresses Isaac Bell's deep disappointment that Thomas Sinton had written back to say that he could not support the project as he had, "absolutely no faith in my machine or what I am doing."

## John Dunville

Even though ballooning had been largely replaced by motoring and powered flight as the sport of choice for the technically minded adventurer, there was still time for an Ulsterman to create newspaper headlines in a lighter-than-air craft. John Dunville (1866–1929) was born at Redburn House in Holywood, Co Down, the son of a well-known and prosperous whiskey distilling family, which owned the Royal Irish Distillery in Belfast. After leaving Cambridge University he was the political Private Secretary to the Duke of Devonshire from 1890 until 1908 and so moved in influential circles. From the age of 10 he was a keen huntsman but did not take up ballooning until the age of 40. Sports ballooning became a popular pastime for well-to-do sportsmen and women in the Edwardian era. The attraction of the sport is evocatively described by Frederick Sykes:

"We sometimes allowed ourselves the experience of 'free trailing' across country with the wind. This involved dragging a hemp rope on the ground from the basket, the length and weight of the rope being such as to keep the balloon at a more or less even height. But crossing telegraph wires and woods led to considerable complications. We were, of course, completely at the mercy of the wind, and a change of direction often occurred at every few hundred yards. We also had some pleasant but chilly night ascents, but the most enjoyable and instructive experiences were on 'free runs'. The stillness and serenity of moving as a part of the wind at a great height above the earth gave pure delight. I loved to look down at the vast map of real country, the downs, and fields and woods, the rivers and pastures and hills of England. The landscape was like a huge bowl gently curving up to a hazy horizon rim. This was one of the things which never lost its charm for me when flying years later, but, though the noise and rush of wind and the cold in an open aeroplane gave a sense of speed, there was much less enchantment than in ballooning."[38]

John Dunville became a prominent member of the Aero Clubs of Ireland and the United Kingdom, taking delivery of his own balloon (manufactured at Eustace and Oswald Short's balloon factory at Battersea) in 1907. On 9 December 1907

John Dunville in the basket of *Banshee*, probably photographed under the Battersea Railway Arch, the Short Brothers' Balloon Factory. *(Michael Clarke Collection)*

Mrs Violet Dunville
with balloon. *(Michael
Clarke Collection)*

he was awarded the ninth Aeronaut's Licence to be issued by the Aero Club of the United Kingdom. The Aero Club was founded on 29 October 1901 and became the Royal Aero Club on 15 February 1910. Flying a balloon was not simply a question of ascending; travelling whither the wind would send you and then descending with a bump to the earth. Aeronauts needed to be able to search for favourable air streams at various heights and to control the jettisoning of ballast and the valving of gas, husbanding these for the longest possible flight. On 11 August 1908 he flew across the English Channel, which was probably about the 50th occasion that this feat had been achieved by balloon since Blanchard and Jeffries on 7 January 1785. In October he flew from Berlin to the German-Danish border, staying in the air for 36 hours and 54 minutes, the longest duration flight by a British-built balloon up to that date. Dunville's balloon, *Banshee*, was state-of-the-art, with a wicker-work 'car' or basket which was carpeted, padded and equipped with electric light. It was not, however, particularly spacious, being 5 feet 3 inches (1.6m) long, 4 feet 8 inches (1.4m) wide and 3 feet six inches (0.76m) deep. Before the end of the year he crossed the English Channel again twice, with three passengers including Dunville's wife, Violet (1861–1940), who was born in Co Meath and was a noted balloonist herself. She later claimed to have been the third lady to have flown the Channel by balloon. In 1909 he was moved to write the following letter to *Flight* magazine:

> "Sir, - I noticed that in the list of cross-Channel voyages made by balloons which was published in *Flight* a few weeks ago, my crossing in the "Banshee" of December 11th 1908, was omitted. This voyage was of some interest as it constituted a record distance from London by a member of the Aero Club. I left Battersea at 9.15 pm, December 11th, and descended to Crailsheim in Wurtemburg, 10.15 am, December 12th, a distance of 485 miles in 13 hours. Further, my crossing of the Channel was the fastest ever made. I noticed that the *Daily Mail* claimed that Blériot's crossing was the fastest ever done, which is incorrect. I left the English coast at New Romney and reached the French coast at Boulogne. From these two points the distance is 35 miles, and my crossing occupied 37 minutes, which is at a rate of 56 4/5 miles per hour! This was the third occasion on which I crossed the Channel by balloon."[39]

Early in 1910 he attempted to cross the Irish Sea in the *Banshee* but suffered a split envelope which resulted in a swift abandonment of the idea. Undeterred, and using the French-built *St Louis*, on 15 February 1910 he flew from the Gasworks in Dublin to Macclesfield in five hours at an altitude up to 10000 feet (3048m) and a speed of 34 mph (54 kph). This was only the third crossing from Ireland to Great Britain after Windham Sadler (1796–1824)

---

39 *Flight*, 18 September 1909

on 22 July 1817 from Portobello (now Cathal Brugha) Barracks, Dublin to Holyhead and John Hodsman (d1903) on 22 April 1867.[40] Dunville's companion was Charles Pollock (c1860–1929), a founding member of the Aero Club and the holder of Aeronaut's Licence No 1, who had informed *Flight* magazine in the same issue as Dunville's letter that he had made no less than 11 crossings of the English Channel by balloon between 1897 and 1909. Violet Dunville had every intention of being on the flight but at the last moment it was decided that taking a third occupant was just too risky in the prevailing wind conditions. Safety had been carefully considered, the basket was covered with a canvas bag to make it more waterproof and a canvas bailing tube was added to the equipment which also included personal floatation gear and a sheet anchor to slow down the passage of the basket if it had to land on water. 900 lbs (408 kg) of ballast, a trail rope, grapple lines, lunch baskets and luggage were also taken on board. The filling by gas and the ascent of the balloon from Dublin in 1910 was supervised by Eustace Short. Dunville described the voyage as follows:

> "We had a very pleasant trip across the Irish Sea. In fact it was so warm the heavy coat which I wore at the start. About four miles from Holyhead we sighted two large cargo steamers. The balloon was dropping a little at the time, and those on board the steamers evidently thought she was in distress and that we required assistance. The ships were turned round, and they stood by with their heads to the wind and their whistles blowing until it was seen that we had reached the land. After that we experienced a very severe snow storm. The balloon was then 8500 feet from the earth and the cold was intense. There were 27 degrees of frost. We had some Perrier water for drinking and at that time the water was freezing in the glass."[41]

A balloon journey card of 1909 for CF Pollock, John Dunville and The Hon Mrs Assheton Harbord, undertaken in the *Valkyrie* at Chelsea. *(Michael Clarke Collection)*

The aeronauts passed by Birkenhead and Liverpool, reaching a maximum height of 10000 feet (3048m). They did not wish to cross into the Peak District, where landing would have been very dangerous, so Dunville opened the valve a little to release some gas. The balloon descended steadily in the strong wind, coming down close to ground level in 18 minutes. He saw the town of Macclesfield in front of them and decided to land:

> "I saw a large grass field with a line of trees on the near side of it, and dropped the balloon down over the trees. When we got within 25 feet of the ground, and in the shelter of the trees, I dropped the anchor, and when she was within 10 feet

---

40  *The Nation,* 27 April 1867 reported that Mr Hodsman, who was a well-known aeronaut, had taken off in his balloon *The Raven* from the Exhibition Palace grounds in Dublin on 22 April and had alighted some hours later near Appleby in Westmorland. It would appear that this was an involuntary crossing of the Irish Sea as he had made no provision for suitable clothing, foodstuffs or india-rubber air cushions to fix around the car of his balloon and render it a tolerably efficient lifeboat.

41  *Belfast Evening Telegraph,* 16 February 1910

of the ground I pulled the pull-rope, and she came down at once and bumped off the ground. Immediately after we got down a tremendous squall swept across the country. If that had caught us we should have had great difficulty in descending."[42]

The balloon was packed up and sent on the train to London, Dunville also went by rail to Holyhead and was back in Dublin by 6 o'clock the next morning.

Dunville maintained his enthusiasm for ballooning until the outbreak of war in 1914 and was soon putting his expertise to use. He joined the Royal Naval Air Service and was appointed as an instructor at No 1 Balloon Training Wing at Roehampton, where not only observation balloon crews but also naval airship pilots at the RNAS Airship Training Station, Wormwood Scrubs, profited from his skills but also from his "ideal blend of kindness and strictness". Airship pilots had to obtain an Aeronaut's Certificate for which they needed to have undertaken two solo flights in a balloon, one by day and one by night. Violet also served, helping to run the canteen for the young officers at Wormwood Scrubs.

Dunville rose to the rank of Squadron Commander, contributed to the development of the highly successful SS class of airship and was awarded the CBE in 1919. Transferring to the RAF when the RNAS was absorbed in 1918, he had the distinction of commissioned rank in all three services, as he was also a Lieutenant Colonel in the Meath Militia (the family had a large country house near Navan in Co Meath). After the war he resumed competitive ballooning but was also an Honorary Wing Commander with No 502 (Ulster) Squadron, with special responsibility for recruiting, from 1926 until his death in 1929. The editor of *Aeroplane* magazine, CG Grey, described his friend as a fine sportsman and a man of money who used his wealth for the public good, as well as being one of the most popular members of White's Club; "few men in clubland have more friends".[43]

James Sadler's ascent from Dublin on 1 October 1812. (*Author's Collection*)

As far as can be reasonably ascertained the first manned balloon ascent in Ireland was on 15 April 1784, by a M Rosseau, accompanied by a drummer boy, from a field at Navan, landing some 90 minutes later near Ratoath, in the same county, Meath. Just over a year later, on 10 May 1785, an accident with a hot air balloon resulted in a fire which destroyed over 100 houses in the town of Tullamore in King's County, thankfully without fatalities. The first aeronaut to fly a balloon in Belfast was Edmund Livingston on Monday, 7 June 1824 from North Queen Street Barracks – home of 11th Regiment of Foot. The *Belfast News Letter* reported that:

42  Ibid
43  *Aeroplane*, 12 June 1929

Sea View House.
(via Maud Hamill)

Richard Crosbie.
(Author's Collection)

"He boldly ascended the car, and the gas-filled balloon at nine minutes past eight o'clock rose majestically over the assembled crowd and slowly floated through the clear atmosphere towards the Cave Hill… Mr Livingston descended with safety in a field belonging to Mr Boomer at Sea View, where the Marquess of Donegall[44] rode over to greet him… They were both hoisted into the balloon basket and carried on the shoulders of the crowd back into town."[45]

Livingston was a friend of Windham Sadler and had planned to accompany him across the Irish Sea in 1817. Other balloonists of note in Ireland included the Wicklow-born Richard Crosbie (1755–1800) who, in 1785, made the first attempt to cross the Irish Sea and Windham's father, James Sadler (1751–1828), who also made an unsuccessful effort in October 1812.

---

44 George Augustus Chichester, 2nd Marquess of Donegall (1769–1844)
45 *Belfast News Letter*, 8 June 1824

Chapter 2

# Record Breakers and Showmen: 1910

THE NEXT FOUR YEARS before the outbreak of the First World War brought a number of daring record breakers and showmen to perform aerial feats which were reported in the local press. In Ireland they included in 1910: the self-styled 'Captain' Cecil Clayton (1870–1958) (no Royal Aero Club Certificate) who exhibited his 30 hp (22 kW) Blériot monoplane in Ballymoney in Co Antrim on 24 June and James Radley (1884–1959) (RAeC Certificate holder No 12, 14 June 1910) at Bangor, Co Down in August, with a 25 hp (18 kW) Blériot, who took off in poor weather as the crowd was demanding that he should fly but unfortunately almost immediately crashed into a tree. One was a highly competent airman; the other was seriously deficient in flying skills.

Captain Clayton
*(David and Kay Cawsey)*

## Ballymoney

Cecil Clayton, whose real name Ernest Charles Clayden was born at Clavering, Essex, in 1870. His uncle, Thomas Wright (1832–1912) had been a professional photographer but also a balloonist of some note, primarily giving exhibitions at the Crystal Palace. He became an actor and subsequently a theatrical manager and impresario, owning the Grand Theatre in Mansfield, Nottinghamshire. The following extract from a newspaper interview[1] of 1911 would tend to give the reader the impression that he was somewhat prone to exaggeration:

"Captain Clayton is an amiable man, with a ready wit and that confidence which one imagined is so necessary to the performance of his daring feats. Well-built, of medium height, he is one who looks as though the world had treated him well. Every feature betokens an endowment of self-confidence, a nature that knows no fear, and a steady determination to overcome every obstacle. It was apparent from the facile way in which he replied to questions touching the event that Captain Clayton possesses that qualification which is essential to those who undertake perilous feats – the ability to decide immediately what is to be done under any circumstances. He gives one the impression that he would never come to grief through hesitating; and it is this, perhaps, which accounts for his escaping any

Clayton with his Blériot at Tiverton in North Devon. *(David and Kay Cawsey)*

A contemporary advert in the local newspaper, the *Coleraine Chronicle*. *(Author's Collection)*

**BALLYMONEY SHOW,**
FRIDAY, 24th JUNE, 1910.

# Aeroplane Exhibition

### By Captain Clayton (Mansfield, Notts.),
PUPIL OF M. BLERIOT.

THE AVIATOR WILL BE PRESENT WITH HIS
## "BLERIOT" MONOPLANE,
which will be on exhibition during the day. He will at intervals fully explain the working of the Machine, and later will proceed to suitable grounds about half-a-mile from town, where Flights will be made, weather and other conditions permitting.

This Machine is an exact duplicate of the Machine with which M. BLERIOT, the famous French Aviator, crossed the Channel last July—the first man to fly a heavier than air Machine across the sea.

Cheap Combined Railway and Show Tickets from all Stations on the Midland Railway (N.C.C.) Line.

serious accident throughout his long career, having made over 1000 balloon ascents, nearly 400 parachute descents, and a succession of brilliant flights!"

It is claimed that he was the first person in England to own a Blériot monoplane, taking lessons at the Blériot Training School, Pau in late 1909. He was not awarded an Aéro-Club de France Aviator's Certificate; however, this deficiency did not stop him importing his aeroplane, tail number 16, to England. Nor, in the spring of 1910, did it prevent him offering to provide flying displays at agricultural and other countryside shows. There was a ready and enthusiastic market willing to pay to see the new phenomenon, so no doubt Clayton saw this as an opportunity for his entrepreneurial spirit.

He was due to appear on Whit Monday 1910 at the Mansfield Agricultural Show, but on the preceding Saturday he had the first of his crashes, seriously damaging the Blériot. His appearance at Worcester on 9 June 1910 was a disaster. A trial flight on the Wednesday preceding the show resulted in a heavy landing resulting in a sprained ankle for Clayton. So the pilot for the attempted flight at the show itself was Clayton's mechanic, Ernest Dartigan (whose real name was Beresford). He had been a circus entertainer with a daring loop-the-loop cycle act, which was probably his only 'relevant' aeronautical experience. The monoplane veered into the crowd, killing a lady by the name of Mrs Ellen Pitt and injuring other spectators. The inquest jury in returning a verdict of Accidental Death, censured Clayton and Dartigan, as well as the Show's organizers for not carrying out a check of their credentials. The incident also led to an article in *Flight* referring to pseudo-aviators who should not be allowed to endanger the public, also adding, "it is becoming the fashion to consider any open-air function incomplete unless there is an exhibition of flying to give tone to it" and concluding that, "none but amply competent aviators be allowed to give these public exhibitions."[2] Ulster aeronaut, John Dunville, was present at the inquest, representing

2 *Flight,* 18 June 1910

the Royal Aero Club and gave his opinion that the narrow space available at Worcester was inadequate to secure safety and that the Club had no official knowledge of either Clayton or Dartigan.[3] Another airman born in Ireland, George Dawes (who will feature later in this account) was also there and endorsed Dunville's remarks.[4] At a committee meeting of the Royal Aero Club on 29 September 1910 it was resolved unanimously that:

> "Any aviator taking part in a public exhibition of flying without having obtained an Aviator's Certificate will render himself liable to having the granting of his Certificate postponed for such a period as the Committee of the Royal Aero Club may determine."[5]

The High Street, Ballymoney in the early twentieth century. *(via Keith Beattie)*

Clayton was invited to exhibit his aeroplane at the North Antrim Agricultural Show in the small Ulster market town of Ballymoney, which was certainly a bold and innovative initiative by the Show Committee. Only a week after the inquest in Worcester he brought his aircraft across to Ireland on the ferry. Unfortunately on the day in question:

"A good deal of interest was aroused by the announcement that Captain Clayton, of Mansfield, Nottinghamshire, would be in attendance at the North Antrim Show at Model Farm, Ballymoney on 24th June 1910 for the purpose – weather conditions permitting, of giving a demonstration of aviation in his Blériot monoplane. He was unable, however, owing to the strong breeze and drenching rain prevailing to fulfil this part of the programme. However, the well-known aviator demonstrated to the visitors the possibilities of the machine, which was housed in a large tent, and during the afternoon was inspected by many interested in this new and attractive, but apparently somewhat perilous, sport. Captain Clayton, who has had fifteen years' experience of ballooning and four of aeroplaning, and has made several flights, explained the mechanism of the monoplane, which is fitted with a three-cylinder engine of 30 horse-power."[6]

The reference to his ballooning and aeroplaning experience would seem to the author to be another example of Cecil Clayton's fairly easy relationship with the exact truth. However, all was not lost:

3  Ibid, 25 June 1910
4  *The Times,* 18 June 1910
5  *The Fellowship of the Air*, p97
6  *Ballymena Weekly Telegraph,* 2 July 1910

*Agricultural Show Grounds, Ballymoney.*

The Agricultural Show
Grounds, Ballymoney.
*(via Keith Beattie)*

"On Friday evening, at the conclusion of the North Antrim Show at Ballymoney,
Captain Clayton, with, his assistant, Mr Dartigan, proceeded about two miles from
Ballymoney to the townland of Druckendult, according to arrangements, and in a
couple of large fields on the farm of Mr James Biggans, on which a splendid course
had been prepared, attempted several flights with his aeroplane, which had been
on exhibition during the day. The weather had much improved from earlier in the
day. The operations were witnessed by a large number of interested spectators from
Ballymoney, Ballycastle, Coleraine, and the surrounding districts. Shortly after eight
o'clock the course, which was admirably suited to the attempt, was cleared, and Mr
Dartigan sped along the ground at about 30 miles an hour on the machine for a
distance of about 500 yards, but without success. Another attempt proved futile.

Captain Clayton then took his seat in the machine and rose to a height of forty feet
the aeroplane continuing on her way for 250 yards amidst loud applause. Captain
Clayton remained over until this morning in Ballymoney, and had another trial at
Druckendult, but the engine of the aeroplane was not in good working order, the rain
having interfered with it during the night and another flight was not attempted."[7]

He later claimed to have been the first man to fly in Ireland, which, of course, can easily be
refuted. Clayton returned to Ireland twice in 1910. In July 1910 the *Southern Star* reported
that Captain Clayton, having travelled on the boat from Liverpool to take part in the New
Ross Agricultural Society Show in Co Wexford, had damaged his monoplane following a
collision with a tree. It had "careened through the fields before lifting briefly to a small
height."[8] Special extra trains had been run from Dublin, Waterford and Wexford, with an
estimated crowd of 6000 being present. Then in August he visited Co Cork at the invitation
of the Clonakility Agricultural Society which was holding its annual Sports Meeting. The

---

7   Ibid
8   *Southern Star,* July 30 1910

*Skibbereen Eagle* described what took place on Saturday, 20 August, at the newly advertised Aviation and Sports Meeting, "The world-renowned Captain Clayton – procured at enormous expense, failed to fly despite several attempts. At five o'clock the machine was brought out and Captain Clayton went on his way amidst the ringing cheers of the vast multitude assembled,"[9] which the paper described as very fashionable, including the 4th Earl and Countess of Bandon (whose cousin and successor as 5th Earl, Paddy, would rise to the rank of Air Chief Marshal in the RAF).

> "He was the recipient of their good wishes and the wonderful invention was set in motion. After several attempts it failed to conquer the air but the gallant Captain and his mechanic repeated their efforts for about two hours and did everything possible to ascend. Only on one occasion did he succeed in leaving the ground and that only for a distance of 20 feet."[10]

Clayton performed at shows in Gloucestershire and North Devon in 1911 and thereafter it would seem that he took no further part in public performances of his flying skills. He died in 1958.

## Bangor

By contrast James Radley viewed aviation as a sporting activity rather than as a business opportunity. He was born in 1884 at Dunnow Hall in Lancashire, the son of a wealthy colliery owner. Before gaining his Aviator's Certificate No12 on 14 June 1910, he was a racing motorist of some note. Radley's name appeared with some frequency in *Flight* magazine in 1910, making a name for himself as a daring and skilful flyer in his Blériot XI. In the course of the summer he had already displayed his aeroplane at Bedford, Bournemouth, Wolverhampton, Pollokshaw (near Glasgow) and Lanark before coming over to Belfast.

A 40 hp Hanriot flown by Rene Hanriot at the Lanark meeting in August 1910.
*(Jack McCleery)*

The show at Lanark Racecourse held in the first two weeks of August was particularly prestigious. Billed as the first flying meeting in Scotland, it was attended by many of the best known airmen of the day including, Cecil Grace, Samuel Cody[11], Captain Bertram Dickson and Armstrong Drexel. A considerable amount of prize money was at stake in 11 different categories of competition. Radley acquitted himself extremely well. Over the six days when he took part he won a total of £1170 and well-merited the acclaim given to him as one of the

---

9   *Skibbereen Eagle,* 27 August 1910
10  Ibid
11  The US-born showman and pioneer, Samuel Franklin Cowdery (later Cody) (1867–1913) made the first officially recognised aeroplane flight in Great Britain on 16 October 1908.

most promising of the newer aviators. He excelled in the daily speed competition of five laps round a 1¾ mile (2.8 km) circuit. He lapped consistently at over 55 mph (88 kph) and flew a straight measured mile at a speed of 75 mph (120 kph). It is not surprising therefore that the local newspaper applauded his arrival at Donegal Quay in Belfast on 26 August 1910:

"There was considerable stir at the quays this morning when large crowds gathered to await the arrival of the Liverpool steamer *Graphic* (Captain J Paisley), the question that excited the curiosity of the large throng being, 'Will the airship arrive' It did arrive, in a taut and trim case of huge dimensions, bearing on the sides, in large stencilled letters, the name of the consigees, LD Gibbs & Co, while at either end was the significant wording, 'Radley, for America'. The significance of the latter consisted in the fact that Radley has been chosen by the Royal Aero Club to represent Britain in the great international for the Gordon Bennett Aviation Cup to be held in the United States next October."[12]

James Radley. *(via Terry Mace)*

He had been booked to display at Bangor, Co Down "a very ancient town and the principal sea bathing resort of the North of Ireland"[13] on the shore of Belfast Lough. The full story was told in another local newspaper:

"Bangor's first pageant: the object, the provision of funds for Bangor new Hospital – was one that appealed to all. It was planned on a scale never before attempted in Bangor. There rallied to its aid a host of volunteer workers, determined that, as far as 'their efforts went, nothing should be lacking. It was the annual trades' holiday in Belfast, and the facilities afforded by the Belfast and County Down Railway Co, in the shape of combined tickets that covered railway fare and admission to the grounds, drew the big majority of pleasure-seekers towards Bangor. The traffic manager, Mr CA Moore, had arranged a special-service of through trains, marshalling all available rolling-stock for the purpose, and, despite the weather, the rush on the line was the biggest since the Twelfth demonstration at Holywood. [Excursion fares including admission to the Grounds were 1st Class 2 shillings, 2nd Class 1/9 and 3rd Class 1/6. The entertainment included the Band of the Royal Irish Constabulary (Belfast), a Trades Procession, a Comic Football Match, a Marathon Race from Belfast, a Prize Boxing Contest, the Balmoral Industrial School Band and Barrett's Royal Nomads – over whom time has sadly drawn a veil].

Three Blériots at Lanark in 1910, one of which may be Radley's. *(via Helen Schofield)*

12 *Belfast Evening Telegraph,* 26 August 1910
13 *Belfast and Ulster Towns Directory,* 1910

Bangor 1910 James
Radley from the *Belfast
Evening Telegraph*.
*(Central Newspaper
Library, Belfast)*

RADLEY'S FLIGHT AT BANGOR.

AFTER THE START.

But to the big majority of the crowd that thronged the demesne at Bangor Castle in the afternoon all the other items were mere sideshows as compared to the chance of witnessing a flight. The announcement that a crack aviator had been engaged was the real lure that made for the success of the pageant, and the bewildering chops and changes, rumours and denials, of the last week had done nothing to take the edge off public interest. At first it was to have been Claude Grahame-White, then when he could not come, Cecil Grace was booked as the star. But here, too, difficulties arose, and at the last moment Radley, who made his mark at Lanark as an airman with few rivals for pluck, stepped into the gap. So many had been the disappointments that it was a relief to see conspicuous on a hillside on the grounds the huge case like a furniture van that housed the machine, and in a specially erected marquee the Blériot monoplane itself ready for action.

A few doubting souls, mindful of the adage about the horse and the water, pointed out that a monoplane in a hangar was a different thing from a monoplane in the air, and openly prophesied there would be no flight. Nor did one need to be an expert to see that they had good grounds for their scepticism. Bangor Castle grounds make a charming background for a "fete champetre," but they have their drawbacks considered as an aerodrome. Trees, loathed by the aviator as barbed wire is by fox hunter, block the outlook on every side, and, though the monoplane had been pitched on the crest of an open hill, clumps of beeches and alders in the valley below gave the flier a poor chance of taking off without a collision. The rough grass was another drawback, for, as Radley pointed out, before he could get up sufficient speed to carry him clear of obstacles his wheels would in all probability be crumpled up like paper. These difficulties might have been surmounted had the weather been favourable, but the fluky wind that kept all the tree tops, rocking was little calculated to help an aviator.

At twelve o'clock, the hour arranged for the first flight, the weather conditions were absolutely impossible, nor, though the wind had subsided a little by two, were the prospects much more favourable. The crowds, who bore their disappointment well on the whole, began to get a little impatient as the afternoon wore on and so great was the crush to see the machine that, in spite of the efforts of mounted constabulary and a body of horsemen mobilised under Mr M'Kee, it looked more than once as if the pressure; of the rear ranks would drive those in front against the frail machine.

At last after five o'clock, Radley announced that he would attempt a flight. The machine was towed out of the marquee; and the horsemen, riding down the crowd, managed to clear a space on the brow of the hill. Apparently, a big proportion of those present had the vaguest notions of how a monoplane worked, for hundreds streamed downhill, and ranged themselves across the valley right in the track of the machine. No attempt was made to clear them away, for once the engine started the horsemen had enough to do to manage their mounts, and one can only be thankful that the thing ended as well as it did. A few minutes before half-past five the clatter of the engine changed to a purr, and, amidst a roar of "He's off," the wings flashed above the mass of the crowd over the crest. The machine went bounding down hill, dipping and falling like a boat in a heavy sea, and about half-way from the bottom sailed suddenly into the air. Radley was aiming for the biggest gap in the line of the trees, but a puff of wind caught him, and slewed him sideways off his course. The Blériot was going in long jumps like a hoop over rough ground, and for a minute it looked as if two incautious sight-seers who had dashed into its path would have been sacrifices to a new juggernaut car. Fortunately they managed to get clear by inches, and Radley, who was steering magnificently, drove the machine between two beeches that barred his way.

As he skimmed past with a few feet to spare one of his right planes struck a tree trunk, ripping off a huge lump of bark, and a second afterwards the Blériot came to a dead stop, with, in addition to its buckled plane, a couple of wheels damaged. Fortunately the injuries were not serious, and Radley escaped without hurt, but it put an end to any further display. In all the machine travelled only between three and four hundred yards."[14]

**PUBLIC NOTICES.**

TO-DAY.

**BANGOR PAGEANT AND FETE**

SATURDAY, AUGUST 27.

PROCEEDS IN AID OF THE BANGOR NEW HOSPITAL.

Owing to unforeseen circumstances,

**R A D L E Y ,**

THE FAMOUS AVIATOR,

WHO IS GOING TO AMERICA IN OCTOBER TO COMPETE FOR THE GORDON BENNETT CUP.

will Fly, in place of GRACE, in the

**BANGOR CASTLE GROUNDS**

(Kindly lent for the occasion by Lady Clanmorris).

By kind permission of the City Commissioner the Splendid BAND OF THE ROYAL IRISH CONSTABULARY (BELFAST), under the direction of Mr. GEORGE C. FERGUSON, will perform during the day.

TRADES PROCESSION. COMIC FOOTBALL MATCH.

GREAT MARATHON RACE FROM BELFAST.

The JEFFRIES-JOHNSON FIGHT by Young's Juvenile Boxing Stars.

The BALMORAL INDUSTRIAL SCHOOL BAND, by kind permission of Mr. D. M'Dowell, will also perform.

BARRETT'S ROYAL NOMADS.

Trams every Twenty Minutes. Fares, including Admission to Grounds—

1st Class, 2/- 2nd Class, 1/9. 3rd Class, 1/6.

Gates (Abbey Street and Castle Street) Open at Twelve o'clock. 4894

A newspaper advert for James Radley's appearance in Bangor. *(Author's Collection)*

The Austrian Alpine Trials 1913, Jimmy Radley and his Rolls-Royce *Silver Ghost* car. *(The Rolls-Royce Heritage Trust)*

In October 1910, as previewed in the *Belfast Evening Telegraph*, he flew in the United States, winning the cross-country aviation race at Belmont Park in New York, covering 20 miles in 19 minutes and 46 seconds, an American speed record. Having become a member of the Royal Aero Club in 1911, he entered the Daily Mail Circuit of Britain Air Race, intending to fly an Antoinette VII monoplane, but he failed to start. In July 1912 he won a cross-country balloon race where he achieved a distance of 132 miles from Hurlingham. For the 1913 Circuit of Britain race, Radley in co-operation with Gordon England (1891–1976) designed and built the Radley-England waterplane, sadly it was damaged before the race and did not complete; the aircraft was subsequently modified and re-built.

He was a friend of 2nd Lieutenant William Rhodes-Moorhouse (1887–1915), the first member of the Royal Flying Corps to be awarded the Victoria Cross, who had started as Radley's mechanic and with whom he formed a company in Huntingdon to design and build aircraft, including the Radley Monoplane of 1911. Maintaining his interest in motoring, in 1912 Radley entered a Rolls-Royce Silver Ghost into the 1912 Austrian Alpine Trial and he also competed in 1913 and 1914. Moreover, in November 1913 he broke the speed record for motoring between London and Monte Carlo, also in a Rolls-Royce Silver Ghost. He died in 1959 at his home at Woodgreen, Hampshire. An obituarist wrote, "With the passing of Jimmy, as he was known to a host of friends, there passed one of the most colourful, cultured and cosmopolitan characters who ever lived."[15]

## Leopardstown – Dickson, Grace, Drexel and Arthur

The Aero Club of Ireland, under the chairmanship of John Dunville, decided to stage the first large air display in Ireland on 29–30 August 1910 at Leopardstown Park Racecourse six miles (9.6 km) south of Dublin, at a cost of £200 for the hire of the venue. The original intention was to invite the very well-known airman Claude Grahame-White (1879–1959) (RAeC Certificate No 6, 26 April 1910), for a fee of £1100 plus free transport of his aeroplane. This plan fell by the wayside following a dispute over the terms of his contract. He was replaced by three others, all equally worthy.

The 'star billing', who would receive a fee of £500 was Captain Bertram Dickson, Royal Artillery and a Fellow of the Royal Geographical Society (1873–1913) (Aéro Club de France Certificate No 71, 19 April 1910). Born in Edinburgh, his career had been adventurous In 1892 he accompanied the geographer Sir Thomas Holdich (1843–1929) to the Andes to define the border between Chile and Argentina, crossing the mountains by mule and also exploring Patagonia. He then served in the British Army, fighting in the Boer War and Somaliland before being seconded for service with the Foreign Office. He had also hunted big game in East Africa and Kurdistan. At the beginning of 1910 he enrolled at the Farman Flying School at Mourmelon "to give his nerves a rest"[16] after he was invalided home from arduous service as Military Consul at Van on the Ottoman-Persian frontier. He was, "in the aviation game for adventure, patriotism and profit in that order."[17] On 6 June 1910 he captured the first world record to be held by an Englishman in his 50 hp (37 kW) Henry Farman III biplane, setting a new mark for the duration of a passenger flight by staying the in the air for exactly two hours, covering 61 miles (98.75 km) in that time.[18] The Farman was a 'pusher' with the engine mounted behind the pilot, who sat atop the lower wing entirely exposed to the elements, within the framework of ash, mahogany and

FLIGHT PIONEERS.

CAPT. BERTRAM DICKSON.

piano wire. Dickson took part in the Lanark flying meet in August 1910, where he won the £400 prize for the greatest aggregate distance flown. He was known for his volplanes:

"…really beautiful pieces of work, he would climb about 1000 feet right over the aerodrome, switch off his engine and then, with his propeller motionless, come stealing slowly and silently down in a series of perfectly judged circles, coming nearer and nearer the popular enclosures until he brought his machine to rest within a few yards of the rails. It was a trick which in the showman's phrase, simply brought down the house."[19]

The other two pilots each were paid £250. Cecil Grace (1880–1910) (RAeC Certificate No 4, 12 April 1910), a very popular pioneer aviator, "an indefatigable worker with a great zest for living."[20] Though born in Chile, he was of Irish-

*Programme from the Aero Club of Ireland's Leopardstown meeting, 1910. (Royal Irish Automobile Club)*

*Opposite:* A very charming stylised portrait of Captain Bertram Dickson from *Flight* magazine of 16 July 1910. *(Flight)*

16  *Bristol Fashion,* p35
17  Ibid p35
18  The brothers Maurice (1877–1964) and Henry (1873–1958) Farman were born of British parents domiciled in Paris. Their aircraft designs were of seminal importance in the development of aviation in Europe.
19  *Ace Air Reporter,* p99
20  *The Fellowship of the Air,* p99

Captain Bertram Dixon
on his Farman biplane.
*(Royal Irish Automobile
Club)*

Cecil Grace 'at the helm of his Short biplane'.
*(Author's Collection)*

American ancestry and from a wealthy, elite family. He began flying in 1909, learning on Moore-Brabazon's Voisin and had recently carried out test pilot duties with Short Brothers at Eastchurch, causing something of a stir in his Short Biplane No 29, "with a flight from Eastchurch over the hills to Sheerness, where he circled above the battleships *Victorious* and *Bulwark* in a manner which gave the Lords of the Admiralty furiously to think."[21] During the event he stayed with his cousin, Sir Valentine Grace at Boley House, Monkstown, Co Dublin. Dickson also stayed in Monkstown with his friend, Colonel Courtenay.

The third airman had to book in at the Hibernian Hotel in Dublin, John Armstrong Drexel (1891–1958) (RAeC Certificate No 14, 21 June 1910), was an American who, on 12 August 1910, set the world altitude record of 6750 feet (2057m) in his 50 hp (37 kW) Blériot at Lanark. This altitude was confirmed by the carefully tested barograph carried in Drexel's monoplane. He has been described as a flamboyant millionaire from Pennsylvania and was the grandson of Anthony J Drexel, a wealthy banker and founder of Drexel University.

21  *History of British Aviation*, p48

THE IRISH TIMES, MONDAY, AUGUST 29, 1910.

PLAN OF THE LEOPARDSTOWN AVIATION COURSE.

Contemporary plan of the 1910 Leopardstown 'Aviation Meeting'. (Author's Collection)

Armstrong Drexel. (Author's Collection)

The Aero Club prepared the ground by erecting a temporary hangar for each of the three airmen; the grass racetrack, from which the course rails had been removed, would be used for take-off and landing, while the existing grandstands would accommodate the anticipated crowds. The aircraft were shipped to Dublin, two Blériots for Drexel, one of which was a 60 hp (44 kW) two-seater and a 50 hp (37 kW) Farman apiece for Dickson and Grace. One report described a horse-drawn removal van trundling along Dublin's Grafton Street with a tarpaulin-covered load marked 'aeroplane' and 'Blériot'.[22] After his machines were reassembled on Sunday, 28 August, Drexel decided to fly his single-seater to Powerscourt in Co Wicklow, where he had been invited to lunch by Viscount Powerscourt, a distance of about 10 miles (16 km) as the crow flies. The *Irish Times* reported:

"He started off in good style, the machine rising from the ground at about 30 yards. Drexel made one circuit of the aerodrome, and then another, at the end of which he descended at his original starting point. He stated that the wind was blowing so strongly across the course that he could not get to the necessary altitude although he had his elevators as advanced as far as possible. The flight lasted five or six minutes and the distance covered was about four miles. The ascent and descent were both neatly accomplished and the monoplane looked extremely graceful

22  *Foxrock Miscellany*, p2

in the air. While Drexel was in the air a train arrived at Foxrock Station and the passengers were all greatly excited at the unexpected sight. Leaving their seats in order to get a view, the stationmaster, Mr Farrell, was compelled to hold the train for a few minutes until the excitement subsided. Lord Powerscourt had anticipated his guest's intention, and had had some trees cut down in order to give a clear landing space for the aviator."[23]

Drexel's brief experience was a foretaste of what the airmen would have to overcome during the Meeting, adverse weather conditions on a site which was not ideal for flying, as the encircling grandstands created turbulence in a space further enclosed by trees and wire fences bedded in concrete. However, on the Monday the crowds flocked to see the show in considerable numbers by train, motor car, bicycle and horse drawn transport. The entrance charge for cars and motorcycles and five shillings, which also gave access to the stands and better access to the aeroplanes; for bicycles and pedestrians it was half a crown and a place in the public enclosure. Countless others tried to watch for free from roads and fields nearby; they climbed trees and posts, clambered onto railway carriage roofs and assembled on Three Rock Mountain to the south-west and Killiney Hill to the east. Many newspapers and journals across Great Britain and Ireland reported on the events of the day including *Flight* magazine which noted that:

> "A long continuous of public conveyances wended its way to Leopardstown, each vehicle carrying its full complement of passengers. During the entire morning the sheds were besieged by spectators anxious to get a glimpse of the machines at close quarters and to ask questions of those who found fame in the flying of them."[24]

The crowd in front of Drexel's hangar. *(Royal Irish Automobile Club)*

23  *Irish Times,* 29 August 1910
24  *Flight,* 3 September 1910

Grace's Farman outside his hangar at Leopardstown. *(Royal Irish Automobile Club)*

To which *The Times* added in a style mixing praise and a somewhat patronizing tone:

"It required considerable courage on the part of the organizers and public-spirited liberality on the part of the guarantors to bring the idea of a flying meeting in Ireland to fruition, in view of the record of financial loss which has been a characteristic feature of similar ventures in Great Britain, and the Aero Club of Ireland is to be congratulated upon the opportunity afforded yesterday to thousands of Irishmen of seeing exhibitions of flying by some of the best experts. Picturesque as is the background of hills under which Leopardstown lies, the place is not an ideal flying centre, for though the surface may be quite free from wind, as was the case yesterday, the upper air gathers currents from the surrounding heights, and both Mr Grace and Mr Drexel considered it unsafe on this account to take up passengers, as had been arranged – a decision which, though no doubt wise and inevitable, caused no little disappointment, as in the absence of competitions passenger-carrying would have provided some slight variation of interest.

There was quite a good attendance, probably between 15 and 20 thousand people paying the half-crown charged for admission to the course. Mr Grace had the honour of being the first to take the air. He was riding a Farman biplane, and after rising easily and with elegance he circled round the course in a flight of short duration and descended on even wheel at his starting point. Mr Drexel then started in his Blériot monoplane, which in appearance and movement found more favour with the spectators than the more cumbrous biplanes. The flying calls for little comment, as the airmen did not attempt any feats of altitude, speed, or other trial favoured in competitions. Captain Dickson's engine gave trouble, and though he started twice he did not achieve a flight of more than a few yards.

The spectators loudly applauded the flights of Mr Grace and Mr Drexel, but after

Drexel and his Blériot.
*(Royal Irish Automobile Club)*

each had taken the air a couple of times the majority left the course, although two hours still remained before the time advertised for the conclusion of the exhibition. It may be that after the first excitement and interest had passed away the Irishman felt lonely to find himself on a racecourse without galloping horses. It may be remarked that, the horses which were on the course behaved in on exemplary manner under the novel trial of their steadiness, with the exception of the horse of a mounted policeman, which was so fascinated and horrified that it kept its frightened eyes fixed, in a stargazing attitude seldom adopted by a horse, on the new phenomenon, performing gyrations the while which greatly embarrassed its rider."

Desmond Arthur.
*(Author's Collection)*

The report was inaccurate in a few respects. Drexel flew twice, making a number of circuits and also climbing to 1200 feet (365m), as well as flying towards the spectators on Three Rock Mountain and Killiney. Having rectified the problem with contaminated petrol, Dickson went aloft late in the day, landing by a glide at a very steep angle. Cecil Grace had to cut short his first flight owing to the securing strip on the back of his seat coming adrift, when he effected repairs and flew again later he did in fact take up a passenger. A young Irishman, 2nd Lieutenant Desmond Arthur, of O'Brien's Bridge, Co Clare, "after much badgering"[25] was taken flying by Grace. After this short hop of 600 yards (550 metres) from which he walked back, as Grace decided that he was too heavy for a return journey, he caught the flying bug, learned to fly and later joined the Royal Flying Corps. It has been claimed that he was the first in Ireland to fly as a passenger. This is not the case as *Flight* noted referring to Harry Ferguson, "as he took up a lady passenger prior to the Leopardstown meeting,

25  www.twosqnassoc.co.uk/pages/stories/ghost/ghost.htm

Drexel in flight over Leopardstown. *(Royal Irish Automobile Club)*

he is justly entitled to the record of having achieved the first passenger flight in Ireland."[26] Indeed if the uncorroborated claim concerning the two Boy Scouts can be proven, then he would be a little further down the list.

Mention should also have been made of the entertainment provided to the crowd by the band of the 1st Battalion of the Rifle Brigade and the marshalling activities of the Hussars and a mounted section of the Royal Irish Constabulary. A 'crash crew' was provided by the horses and water engines of the Pembroke Fire Brigade. The event was also attended by many members of Society, including the Lord Lieutenant of Ireland, the Earl of Aberdeen, with a large Vice-regal entourage, Lord Iveagh, Lord Powerscourt, Mr Justice Wylie, Sir Horace Plunkett and HE Perrin, the Secretary of the RAeC.

On the Monday evening a banquet was given by the Corinthian Club at the Gresham Hotel in Dublin attended by 300 guests and was heralded as the "society event of the year"[27] The airmen made after dinner speeches and praised the Aero Club's organisation of the event.

Unfortunately the weather the following morning was most inclement and prevented any flying before mid-afternoon. Cecil Grace made a short flight in "gusts of winds swayed his machine considerably, and caused it to pitch and roll like a boat on choppy sea."[28] A few months later it was written that, "he made a splendid but, to those who knew, a terrifying flight, over most dangerous ground in a treacherous wind rather than let the crowd go away disappointed."[29] He decided that he would be more safely employed giving some hardy souls

26  Ibid, 8 October 1910
27  *Air Spectaculars*, p18
28  *Flight*, 3 September 1910
29  *The Aero*, 4 January 1911

Cecil Grace prepares to depart on his last flight. *(via Terry Mace)*

CECIL·GRACE. 22.12.10. DOVER.

short hops along the racecourse at a charge of £10 per head. Dickson made a short flight but "finding himself unable to clear some trees made a very skilful landing between two closely set wire fences."[30] Drexel did not fly at all as he was unwell, according to one account.[31] Though according to *The Times*, Captain Dickson, "after flying once round the course came down and informed Mr Drexel, who brought out his monoplane on the course, that further flying was impossible."[32] Overall the event was judged a success, not least because the Aero Club made a profit of £421 after all expenses had been deducted.

Sadly the stars of the Meeting enjoyed very mixed fortunes thereafter. Grace was naturalized as a British citizen in October 1910 and late in the year was one of the entrants competing for the Baron de Forest Prize of £4000 for the longest flight from England into continental Europe. Grace departed Swingate Downs near Dover on 22 December 1910 flying a Short S.27. A telegram was received that Grace had landed near the village of Les Baraques near Calais. Having experienced the adverse nature of the weather conditions, he decided to return to England and try again another day. He was never seen again. On 6 January 1911 a pilot's goggles and cap were washed ashore later identified as Grace's. He was posthumously awarded the Gold Medal of the Royal Aero Club. His obituarist summed Cecil Grace up as follows:

> "His keen grey eyes, powerful jaw and aquiline nose leave in one's memory a mental picture as clear as, and as like to, those portraits of great leaders of men which are the outstanding memories of one's long past lessons in history. Yet, despite this

30  Ibid
31  *Air Spectaculars*, p19
32  *The Times*, 31 August 1910

impression of power, an impression which justified itself in reality, Grace had a quiet, gentle manner which gave him an added charm, and was the outward sign of the kindly heart and studious mind which were so strangely allied to his forceful character and daring spirit."[33]

By September 1910 Dickson had resigned his Army commission to take up a post with the British & Colonial Aircraft Company helping promote their products. On 21 September "the small, trim, black-haired, black-moustached military figure … wisely wrapped in several layers of newspapers beneath his clothes"[34] flew a Bristol Boxkite that took park in the annual British army manoeuvres on Salisbury Plain, somewhat against the wishes of the top brass, particularly those with a cavalry background. Dickson located 'Blue Force', then landed and reported back to 'Red Force' headquarters by telephone. Before he could take off again, however, he was captured by Corporal Arthur Edwards of the 4th Dragoon Guards, part of 'Blue Force'. While the umpires were discussing how to resolve this unprecedented situation, Dickson happened to meet the Home Secretary, Winston Churchill, who was observing the manoeuvres, and was able to impress on him the importance of aviation to the Army. Having read of these events in the next morning's newspapers, Robert Loraine, a well-known actor and enthusiastic aviator (who will reappear in this story soon) travelled down from London to offer his services to 'Blue Force'. The other Boxkite supplied by Bristol was fitted with a radio transmitter. Loraine combined flying his aircraft using his left hand, while using his right hand to transmit Morse Code messages over a distance of up to a mile

Captain Dickson and Boxkite No 4 during the Army manoeuvres in September 1910. *(Museum of Army Flying)*

---

33  *The Aero* 4 January 1911
34  *Bristol Fashion* p39–40

FIRST COLLISION IN THE AIR.—As the mishap to Capt. Bertram Dickson, on his Henry Farman, when M. Thomas, on his Antoinette, dashed into him from above, at Milan, appeared to A. Beltrame, an Italian artist. This picture appeared in *La Domenica del Corriere*.

Bertram Dickson's unfortunate crash at Milan, 1910. *(Author's Collection)*

to 'Blue Force' headquarters – the first radio signals to be sent from an aeroplane in Britain. These were the first heavier-than-air machines to operate with British military forces. The involvement of the two airmen certainly made a positive impact on military minds which were not closed to new ideas and in all probability hastened the formation of the Air Battalion of the Royal Engineers in 1911.

Sadly only a few days later, on 1 October 1910 while in Milan, Dickson was involved in the first mid-air collision between two aeroplanes; an Antoinette monoplane, piloted by René Thomas (1886–1975)[35] of France, rammed Dickson's Farman. Both pilots were injured in the crash. Although Dickson survived, he never fully recovered from his grave internal injuries, a broken leg, dislocated pelvis and great physical discomfort, requiring a stomach pump every few hours, administered by his valet, which contributed to his early death on 28 September 1913. He was described by his friend and fellow aviator, Howard Pixton[36] (1885–1972) as, "A very charming, aristocratic man who had a passion for flying."[37] He flew as a passenger with Howard Pixton in 1911 from Larkhill, telling *The Aeroplane*, "I'm very pleased with my flight and have great confidence in Pixton as a pilot. I feel scarcely strong enough to control a machine for any length of time, but I certainly hope to do a little flying, now I know how I feel in the air again."[38]

In contrast, Armstrong Drexel survived not only the hazards of pre-war aviation but also considerable exposure to danger on the ground and in the air during the Great War. In 1914 he gave his motor car to the Commander of the British Expeditionary Force, Field Marshal Sir John French, on the understanding that he could act as his chauffeur. He drove Sir John all through the first year, including the Battle of Mons, when it was discovered that he was an American citizen. Subsequently he joined the French Foreign Legion and then flew with the crack French No 124 Escadrille Américaine until 1917.[39] He was subsequently commissioned as a Major in the Aviation Section, US Signal Corps, serving until the end of the war in the United States Army Air Service. He also became only the 8th airman to receive an Aero Club of America pilot's licence.

---

35   Recovered to win the Indianapolis 500 in 1914, driving a Delage.
36   During 1918 Captain Howard Pixton RAF travelled around Ireland surveying suitable sites for airfields and landing grounds. Pixton travelled extensively exploring 76 potential locations in no less than 24 counties.
37   *Howard Pixton – Test Pilot and Pioneer Aviator*, p150
38   Quoted in *Howard Pixton – Test Pilot and Pioneer Aviator*, p100
39   Letter to *The Times*, 13 March 1958

## Robert Loraine

During the course of the meeting at Leopardstown it was known that an attempt was being prepared to fly from Great Britain to Ireland and rumours spread around the crowd that the pilot would land on the course to complete the flight. These hopes were just a little premature. Robert Loraine (1876–1935) had run away from school at the age of 13 to follow his parents, Harry and Nellie, into the theatrical profession – against their wishes. At the turn of the century, he served in the Boer War in South Africa, where he was twice mentioned in dispatches. Loraine was a versatile actor and was successful both in serious plays and in popular works of light entertainment in London and on Broadway. Of him it was later written that, "He had, perhaps by inheritance, the true actor's quality of seeming to be at home and expressive in any sort of part he chose to play."[40] He was particularly associated with the plays of George Bernard Shaw (1856–1950); in fact he induced the great Irish playwright to accompany him on a balloon flight from the Wandsworth Gasworks in London in 1907 to celebrate the success of his play *Man and Superman*.

Robert Loraine – the celebrated actor.
*(Author's Collection)*

In 1909 he decided to learn to fly, firstly at the Blériot School at Pau in the Lower Pyrenees and then more successfully at the Henry Farman School at Mourmelon in north-eastern France, being awarded his Aéro Club de France Certificate No 126 on 21 July 1910. He purchased a 50 hp (37 kW) Farman biplane for £7,000 and engaged the engineer Jules Védrines (1881–1919) as his mechanic. To begin with he used the pseudonym 'Mr Jones'

40  *The Times,* 27 December 1935

Loraine takes off from Penrhos Park on 10 September 1910.
*(Author's Collection)*

when engaged in flying activities. Loraine was a brave pilot but not a particularly skilful one. It is said that Védrines was kept well occupied repairing the machine, following heavy landings and other mishaps. When asked if Loraine was a lunatic or a hero, he answered that he was a bit of both in turn and sometimes both at once.

Shortly after 11.00 am on Sunday, 10 September 1910 Loraine set out from Penrhos Park, Holyhead where, "a large crowd had gathered to see the start and the aviator was heartily cheered as he mounted the seat and got ready for his journey"[41] in his Farman with the intention of being the first aviator to cross the Irish Sea – a distance of over 60 miles (96 km) and a very daunting goal. He did not arrange for a naval escort to accompany him, there were no elaborate preparations, he simply started up his engine, took off, climbed to 4000 feet (1218 m) and steered westward out to sea. After about ten minutes he had disappeared from view. He was observed making good progress by the Royal Mail steamer sailing from Kingstown to Holyhead. On the way across Loraine's engine stopped six times due to an obstruction in the petrol feed and each time he dived over 2000 feet (609 m) in an effort to restart it by 'windmilling' the engine, intermittently also snapping a bracing wire. This was a hazardous situation as there was the strong likelihood that his craft could simply come apart in the air from the stress of descending and climbing. It is probably that the aircraft had not been re-rigged properly after an earlier accident.[42] Loraine later remarked, "luckily there were plenty of wires on the old Farman."[43] The last time this happened he had to abandon his previous plan to land in Phoenix Park in Dublin and instead alight on the water off Howth Head, "which he had reached either by luck or brilliant navigation"[44] and swim the last 200 feet (69 m) ashore to the Baily lighthouse (some sources say 70 feet (21 m) others 300 yards (275 m) from the shore).

The badge of the Loraine Wheelers Cycle Club which was inspired by his aeroplane's Gnome rotary engine. (via Bob Montgomery)

The Farman had 'turned turtle' on landing so Loraine tumbled out head first and was obliged to dive and swim for some distance underwater.[45] His aeroplane was salvaged by the crew of the SS *Adela,* a three-masted iron steamer launched in 1879 and used on the Dublin to Liverpool service by Tedcastle, McCormick & Co Ltd.[46] Meanwhile Loraine was assisted ashore by members of a local cycle club who were out for a spin. They decided to honour the occasion by adopting the name 'The Loraine Cycling Club', with the good-natured agreement of Loraine himself. Having dried himself off and removed his cork lifebelt, he put off from the lighthouse in a small boat to rendezvous with the *Adela,* examine his aeroplane, which had only suffered

---

41  *Aberdeen Evening Express,* 12 September 1910

42  Broadly speaking the wings of biplanes were braced with two sorts of wires, flying wires and landing wires, arranged diagonally between the upper and lower planes. Flying wires held the wings in position in the air; landing wires took the weight of the wings when the machine was standing on the ground.

43  Quoted in *Early Aviation in Ireland* p36. Farman types were well-known for their multiplicity of wires and were affectionately known as 'bird-cages'. In *Biggles Learns to Fly*, Captain WE Johns quoted one of Biggles' flying instructors advising him, tongue-in-cheek, that the best way to find out if all the wires are in place is to put a canary between the wings; if the bird gets out, you know there is a wire missing somewhere.

44  *History of British Aviation,* p38

45  *The Times,* 12 September 1912

46  The SS *Adela* was torpedoed and sunk by a U-boat off the Skerries on 27 December 1917.

slight damage from its immersion, thank Captain Kinch and his crew, and proceed to Dublin. One of the passengers described the aviator:

> "Apart from the regrets for the unfortunate ending of the flight when within sight of his goal, it was reassuring that the brave airman had escaped with his life. He was full of energy and coolness, anxious only for the safety of his biplane, which had borne him so well on his daring flight, the longest over sea that has ever taken place. Loraine is a man of medium build, muscular and active. He has the typical face of an actor, with a fine forehead, a moulded mouth and a furrow between cheek and lips. When one saw the cool and intrepid manner in which he conducted the salvage of his machine, unexcited and restrained, one felt that Loraine satisfied his pre-conceived notion of the man of the highest courage and determination."[47]

Robert Loraine sitting on his Farman. *(Author's Collection)*

On arrival at Sir John Rogerson's Quay Loraine boarded the mail boat, the SS *Anglia*,[48] for a couple of hours sleep. On awakening he was interviewed by the press and thanked all he had come into contact during his flying visit to Ireland for their kindness and courtesy.[49] He returned to Holyhead that evening in the *Anglia*. The Farman was returned across the Irish Sea to Holyhead by the TSS *Slieve Bloom* of the London and North-Western Railway Company.[50] By an odd coincidence the play in which Loraine was starring at the Queen's Theatre in London was titled *The Man From the Sea* by William J Locke. He was later awarded the Silver Medal of the Royal Aero Club and the approbation, "No pioneer ever attempted a more dangerous task and none ever had so many successive escapes from death in so short a time."[51] *The Times* added that, "Between 1910 and 1912 Loraine made a great number of flights, took part in numerous flying meetings and did good service generally for aeronautics."[52]

He joined the RFC (Military Wing) on 12 August 1914 as a 2nd Lieutenant on probation in the Special Reserve. Loraine's limitations as a pilot were emphasized in 1914 when he was sent to France to serve with No 3 Squadron as an observer, having crashed two aircraft in training. By a remarkable coincidence one of his pilots was Denys Corbett Wilson, another name which will soon feature in this account. On 22 November 1914 Loraine suffered a serious wound from ground fire while on artillery observation duties with Corbett Wilson.

---

47  *Irish Times,* 11 September 1910

48  The SS *Anglia* was requisitioned as a hospital ship during the Great War and was sunk by the UC-5 on 17 November 1915

49  *Irish Independent,* 12 September 1913

50  *Irish Independent,* 13 September 1910. (The TSS *Slieve Bloom* was also sunk in WW1 following a collision with the USS *Stockton* on 31 March 1918)

51  *History of British Aviation,* p38

52  *The Times,* 27 December 1935

*Above:* Robert Loraine in later years. *(via Terry Mace)*

*Above right:* A BE2c, as flown by No 2 Squadron. *(JM Bruce JS Leslie Collection)*

Loraine, with a theatrical flourish, had earlier dropped a note to the Germans, "Keep your eye in, we will be back this afternoon!"[53] True to their word, they were back and spent 45 minutes directing artillery fire while their engine was at full throttle, beating into the persistent east wind, which rendered the virtually motionless Blériot a sitting target. Then a bullet from a shrapnel shell hit Loraine in the back. He later wrote in his diary, "As my reconnaissance was of immediate importance, I tried to continue, but found that details were utterly beyond me. So I asked Corbett Wilson to go back to our landing ground, telling him I was hit. Then, as there was nothing else to do, I fainted."[54] Corbett Wilson wrote to his mother, "Loraine has gone to England; he was shot through the lungs, poor chap, the bullet went through his British warm coat, also through his leather flying jacket, and was found in his shirt. He'll get all right with care. He was quite cheery when I saw him."[55]

After recuperating on a trip to South America, he returned to France in April 1915 only to be recalled soon after for pilot training. He returned to France as a pilot and joined No 2 Squadron flying the BE2c, soon becoming a flight commander. Captain Loraine was awarded the Military Cross for shooting down an Albatros reconnaissance biplane on 26 October 1915, in company with his observer, Lieutenant Eric Lubbock, driving it down from 9000 feet to 600 feet in what the *London Gazette* described as "For conspicuous gallantry and skill."[56]

In March 1916 he was sent, on promotion to Major, to take command of a new squadron, No 40, forming at Gosport in Hampshire. It was equipped with single-seat FE8 fighters and sent to France in August 1916. Loraine was rather a martinet and demanded high standards which made him somewhat disliked by his men. In February 1917 he was promoted again to Lieutenant Colonel, awarded the Distinguished Service Order (DSO) and given command of

53  *Letters from An Early Bird*, p90
54  Ibid p90
55  Ibid p98
56  11450 Supplement to the *London Gazette*, 18 November 1915

No 14 Wing. Later he was posted back to England to command a Training Wing at Andover. His unpopularity increased as he was perceived to be demanding and callous in his attitude to the trainees – however it could be said that he was merely trying to make sure that they faced up to the exacting demands of flying on the Western Front. He was court martialled, under somewhat dubious circumstances, for being drunk on duty, was acquitted and requested to return to active flying duties, reverting voluntarily to Major. He returned to France in May 1918, commanding No 211 Squadron, flying DH9 bombers. In July he was wounded once more and invalided home. Those who served with him rather than under his command, remembered him fondly as an engaging, larger than life, character.

An artist's impression of a No 40 Squadron FE8 being attacked by an Albatros D-III. *(Author's Collection)*

After the war he returned to the stage and continued with his career as both an actor and a theatrical manager, though he also continued to take an interest in flying. In 1920, "He was flying home from St Moritz when he lost his way and came down in a Prussian town, where the attitude of the inhabitants induced him to pass himself off as a Swiss."[57] He died in December 1935 at the age of 59 after an operation for quinsy. *The Times* obituarist noted that, "On the stage he was a gallant and romantic figure, and not less gallant in war and in the perils of early aviation."[58]

A DH9, the type which equipped No 211 Squadron. *(JM Bruce JS Leslie Collection)*

---

57  *The Times*, 27 December 1935
58  Ibid

## Chapter 3
# Interlude:
# 1911

After the excitement of 1910 it was, perhaps, inevitable that the following year would represent something of an anticlimax.

Harry Ferguson's further experiments are described in Chapter 1, while Lilian Bland finished her flirtation with aviation and, as far as is known, no airmen visited Ireland with their machines to entertain the public. The Aero Club in Dublin tried to stimulate progress. *Flight* noted in April that, at its Annual General Meeting, the Club had decided to offer a prize of £100 for the longest distance greater than 25 miles (40 km) flown in Ireland up to 1 October 1911.[1] In the same issue it was recorded that expenditure at the Leopardstown meeting had been £2489.1.0 and receipts £2910.19.9. In the summer *The Motor News* reported on Harry Ferguson:

> "The May Street Garage in Belfast is a well equipped establishment which caters for quite a large number of customers. As the home of the Ferguson aeroplane, it has gained considerable fame. We noticed on a recent visit that the work of reconstructing this monoplane is proceeding apace. The chassis is finished and the main planes are almost ready. It may be remembered that, in order to avoid colliding with some spectators, Mr Ferguson on his last flight [at Magilligan in October 1910] brought his machine heavily to earth. Despite the fact that the major portion of the chassis was riven to splinters, the tail stood the strain without failing – a good testimonial to the quality of the work put into it. In the loft, above the shop, Mr Fraser, of the May Street Garage, showed us the new propeller which had just come to hand. It possesses a pair of finely shaped blades, which, we feel sure, will do their share in demonstrating Ferguson as a most capable flyer. Our Irish aviator has always been handicapped by some shortcoming or other in the equipment of his machine. Let us hope his difficulties have been, this time, better met."[2]

---

1 *Flight,* 1 April 1911

2 *The Motor News* 5 August 1911. By 1911 Harry Ferguson was established at 87 May Street, Belfast in what would eventually be named Harry Ferguson Motors Ltd. It was in these premises that Harry completed the design and construction of the last variant of his aeroplane.

Harry Ferguson's premises in May Street, Belfast. *(Ferguson Family Museum)*

Towards the end of the year a further prize of £25 was offered to the aviator of a machine built in Ireland which made the greatest number of half-mile straight flights between 8.00 am and 4.00 pm on any three days between 20 November and 21 December.[3] A deposit of £5 was required, returnable following a bona fide attempt to fly. It would not appear that these challenges were taken up.

An aviation exhibition, held as part of the Aonach na Nodlag or Christmas Fair (a display of Irish-manufactured products) in the Large Concert Hall of the Rotunda in Dublin, was a popular attraction in December, one of the exhibitors being Harry Ferguson, who brought his monoplane. The Aonach Committee noted that it was indebted to the Great Northern Railway in connection with the carriage of the machine from Belfast to Dublin. The Dublin *Evening Herald* noted that, "The machine is under control in every direction by two hand levers and a foot-bar, all controlled from the pilot seat."[4]

Ferguson's assistant, Sam Turkington, gave a talk on the principles of flying the aeroplane and was supported by series of discourses on aviation from "the pilot seat of Mr Harry Ferguson's Irish-made aeroplane"[5] by Francis JP Jones. In a contemporary newspaper article Jones urged that an Irish aviation industry should be established.[6] Model aeroplanes which were claimed to be capable of making a flight of 200 feet were available for sale at the Aonach at a price of one shilling and "a unique collection of photographs of all the leading aviators decorates the walls of the exhibition room."[7]

---

3  Ibid, 18 November 1911
4  *Evening Herald*, 7 December 1911
5  *Irish Independent*, 7 December 1911
6  Ibid
7  *Freeman's Journal*, 11 December 1911

The Rotunda, Dublin where the Aonach Committee held an aviation exhibition as part of its Christmas Fair. *(Image Courtesy of the National Library of Ireland)*

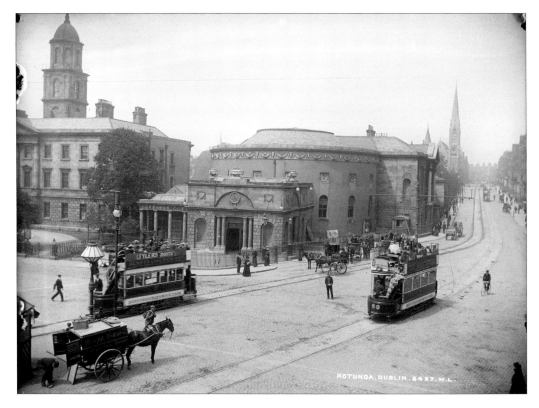

In a major article describing the Aonach's opening ceremony *Freeman's Journal* reported that Irish manufacturers in the last year had, "exported the surprising amount of £26,000,000 of goods, more than £21,000,000 of this went from Belfast, the chief items being £3,500,000 worth of ships, £13,100,000 worth of linen goods, £1,200,000 of linen yarn, £1,400,000 of cotton goods, £500,000 worth of machinery, £460,000 worth of rope cordage and twine, £440,000 worth of thread and £400,000 of tobacco."[8]

That the disappointment of many, with regard to a perceived lack of technological progress in Ireland as a whole, was keenly felt, may be judged from this comment column which appeared in *The Motor News* early in 1912:

IRELAND AND AVIATION

"It is really a great pity that neither the youth of Ireland nor those who have reached man's estate show the slightest interest of a practical nature in aviation. Aviation has now for several years been a popular hobby of a vast number of people in England and on the Continent, yet over here, in the Green Isle, we seem to be content to keep au fait with the subject by an occasional glance at the news reports of flights elsewhere. Of course, we are a poor nation and a farming community, and, of course, the climate is damp (sometimes), and of course we have not got the facilities for studying the rudiments of the science. But none of these references make either sound argument or valid excuse.

8  *Freeman's Journal*, 8 December 1911

MODEL FLYING AND GLIDING CLUBS

And why, because the science and art can be studied and learnt for a negligible cost to each individual participating. All that is required is a little co-ordination, the formation of model-flying clubs and gliding clubs. The subscription need be quite small and, probably, donations would be forthcoming from a number of public-spirited people whose patronage could be sought. Model-flying clubs would have, as members, youths, school-boys, etc., and at once ought to be established in, say, Dublin, Belfast, Cork, and Limerick. As regards gliding clubs, these would draw on persons of all ages; possibly both sexes. There is room for several such clubs in Ireland. Trinity, for instance, should have a special one to itself, and if the students were worth their salt, as the saying goes, they would tackle to at once and see to its formation. It might be thought that the paraphernalia attaching to a gliding club was expensive and difficult to obtain. Not a bit of it, as will be understood when we state that a ten-pound note will purchase all material, plans, designs, etc., necessary for the construction of a glider. From all accounts the amount of genuine enjoyment accruing to membership of a gliding club makes the game well worth the candle."

THE IRISH AERO CLUB

Model-flying and gliding clubs are, just now, necessary adjuncts to an aero club, for they constitute admirable recruiting grounds. We suggest that, if the Irish Aero Club is going to deserve the national title it has assumed, and if it is to be our representative body on matters aerial, then it should do something of a practical nature - something in the way of organising model flying and gliding clubs.

THE IRISH FLYING CLUB

In Dublin we have a new institution, the Irish Flying Club, and perhaps the executive is imbued with a little of the ardour required if any vigour is to be put into the fostering of aviation in Ireland. Yes, in Dublin there are two flying clubs; but Belfast has the honour of possessing the sole Irish aviator in Ireland - though Dublin has several representatives aloft in other lands. The columns of *The Motor News* have consistently been used for the furtherance of Irish flying, and it is a matter of regret to us that our enthusiasm in this regard is well nigh a lone effort and is not the reflection of enterprise shown by our fellow-countrymen."[9]

9 *The Motor News*, 27 January 1912

Chapter 4

# A Momentous Year: 1912

## Corbett Wilson and Allen

ONE WEEK AFTER THE loss of the RMS *Titanic*, on 22 April 1912, the first successful crossing from Great Britain to Ireland by aeroplane was made by the Anglo-Irishman Denys Corbett Wilson (1882–1915) (Aéro Club de France Certificate No 722, 16 January 1912). His father, William Henry Charles 'Carlos' Wilson was a successful barrister, his mother, Ada Caroline, whose maiden name was Corbett, was Irish from Co Kilkenny. Corbett Wilson grew up in comfortable circumstances in Surrey. He was educated at Eton College from 1896 to 1899; subsequently he served in the army in South Africa during the Boer War in the Dorset Regiment, completing his service in 1908 as a Lieutenant in the Royal Artillery. After early death of his father, he lived with his mother firstly in South Africa and then in Ireland at Darver House near Jenkinstown in Co Kilkenny. He enjoyed country pursuits, especially hunting and was known as a quiet, gentle, reticent man, with a love of animals, especially his Scottie, Jock.

Like many wealthy, adventurous young men of his time, he enjoyed driving high-powered cars at speed. It is not surprising, therefore, that he took an interest in the new sport of aviation. In 1911 he enrolled at the Blériot Flying School at Pau. On gaining his certificate he bought himself a single-seat 50 hp (37 kW) Blériot XI. He was a pilot of very limited experience when he determined to fly to Ireland.

The Blériot Flying School at Pau, France. *(via Donal MacCarron)*

He set off from Hendon Aerodrome on the afternoon of 17 April 1912 in a good-natured race against his friend and fellow pilot Damer Leslie Allen (1878–1912). Allen, who was from Limerick, and was a junior partner in a firm of naval architects, was also flying a 50 hp (37 kW) Blériot and had also recently gained his RAeC Certificate, No 183, on 20 February 1912. Allen took a more northerly course than Corbett Wilson and reached Chester that evening, having followed the London and North-Western Railway line and by way of a landing 10 miles from Crewe for 15 minutes to ascertain his whereabouts. Poignantly, he was hailed as the first aviator to land in Chester. On 18 April just after 6.00 am he took off again and was sighted an hour and 50 minutes later above Holyhead steering out to sea. He was never seen again. On 24 June 1912, the High Court in London made an order that Allen should be presumed to have died on or after 18 April 1912. He left an estate valued at £6,923 15s 8d. At the time of his death Allen was being sued in the English courts for the recovery of a portrait of Lady Anne Ponsonby by Thomas Gainsborough, which he had sold at Christie's for 8,300 guineas (£8,715). On 11 February 1913, after a seven-day trial, the jury returned a verdict for the defendants, including the executors of Allen's estate.[1]

Damer Leslie Allen.
*(Author's Collection)*

Meanwhile on 17 April 1912, Corbett Wilson, having lost his compass overboard, landed near Hereford and booked into the Mitre Hotel. Rather than wait for his mechanic to arrive, he decided to purchase petrol and oil locally, as well as a new compass. The oil (castor oil was used at the time) turned out to be the wrong grade and on resuming his flight the following morning he was forced down because of engine trouble. This time he landed in the little village of Colva in Radnorshire where he wisely waited for his mechanic to arrive. It was on 21 April he took off and decided to head west instead of north for Chester and Holyhead as the original plan. He arrived at a field near Harbour Village, Goodwick around mid-morning. The historic flight to Ireland began at 5.47 am on the 22 April, flying across St George's Channel in 1 hour 40 minutes and landing at Crane, two miles from Enniscorthy. It would seem that he had a fairly uneventful crossing until he was only 15 miles (24 km) from making his landfall, later remarking:

Denys Corbett Wilson prepares for his departure from Colva.
*(via Donal MacCarron)*

1 *The Times,* 11 February 1913

After repairs at garage in Enniscorthy, Denys
Corbett's repaired the Blériot is ready to fly again.
*(via Donal MacCarron)*

Landed at Crane after its encounter with a
'good, honest Wexford stone-faced bank'.
*(via Donal MacCarron)*

"I ran into a squall, wind and rain and most unpleasant; whatever height I tried it
was bad. After about 30 minutes of it the motor began to miss; the compass was also
behaving erratically and visibility was bad. I had difficulty in keeping my course.
As it happened I was near land and soon got a glimpse of fields. I staggered on
for another ten miles with a failing engine and I decided to come down. It was
still pouring when I landed and the machine was saturated. The landing chassis
was somewhat damaged in this encounter with a good, honest Wexford stone-faced
bank. I landed in fog and didn't realize the field was so small till too late. However,
very little damage was done."[2]

Corbett Wilson's aeroplane was repaired at a garage in Enniscorthy. He subsequently flew
home to Darver House on a Sunday morning. The distance by air was about 30 miles (50
km). It would appear however that he lost his way and flew more than twice that distance,
right across Co Kilkenny into Co Tipperary, passing over parishioners on their way to Mass
at the village of Fethard. He landed nearby to establish where he was:

2  *Letters from An Early Bird*, p17

"Needless to say, in a district where the nearest railway station was many miles away, and the shriek of a steam engine had never been heard, the unexpected arrival of an aeroplane caused quite a sensation. In a very short time a huge crowd had gathered and all day long a continuous stream of people came to see the flying man and his marvellous machine."[3]

It was evening before he could take his leave of the hospitable people of the district and within an hour he was home. The following morning he gave an impromptu display over Kilkenny, circling the city at 500 feet (152 m). Corbett Wilson was much in demand during 1912 giving flying displays at sports days and agricultural shows across Munster, for example, a few miles from home at Ardaloo on 23 May before a crowd of 5000. In June *The Motor News* reported:

"We have received an interesting letter from Mr W M'Cammond, of Kilkenny, the manager of Messrs Statham & Co's garage. He says that the citizens of that favoured town are almost daily treated to the sight of an aeroplane in flight over the town. Mr Corbett Wilson is the aviator, and it will be remembered that a short time ago he was successful in flying the Channel, being the first pilot to actually reach Ireland by aeroplane. His home is at Darver, about six miles from Kilkenny, and he recently flew from there to Enniscorthy, a distance of 30 miles, in twenty minutes, and gave exhibition flights in aid of a local charity. Three days afterwards he flew back to Darver. Mr Wilson is our most prominent aviator, and he deserves the congratulations of every Irishman on his performances."[4]

However, while flying from Kilkenny to Clonmel on 4 July he landed heavily at Powerscourt in Co Wicklow:

"As a result of the impact my face was cut under the right eye by the corner of the compass frame which smashed one of my lenses [of his goggles]. However I am lucky in having escaped so well."[5]

The Blériot sustained rather more damage to its propeller, undercarriage, fuselage and engine, being returned to the factory at Buc near Paris for

Denys Corbett Wilson at Powerstown.
*(via Donal MacCarron)*

3  Ibid, p23
4  *The Motor News*, 1 June 1912
5  Ibid, p26

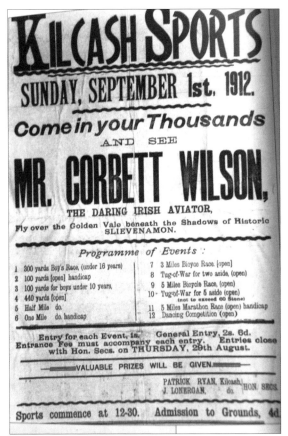

An advertising poster for the Kilkash Sports. *(Author's Collection)*

remedial attention. This was successful as on 1 September it was advertised that he would fly at the Kilcash Sports in Co Tipperary "over the Golden Vale beneath the shadows of historic Slievenamon."[6] He also performed at Clonmel on 9 October, in an event organized by the Clonmel Picture Palaces Association, flying from the racecourse grounds after gracefully circling the town.[7]

## Vivian Hewitt

It has been claimed that the first successful aerial crossing of Irish Sea was made by Vivian Hewitt (1888–1965) (RAeC Certificate No 302, 1 October 1912), again in a Blériot, on 26 April 1912 from Holyhead to Phoenix Park in the heart of Dublin. Strictly speaking this is true, as Robert Loraine's flight terminated in the water and Denys Corbett Wilson flew over St George's Channel. Born in Grimsby, to a very wealthy local family and founders of the Hewitt brewing empire, Vivian parents moved to Bodfari in Flintshire. His father, Titus, was a gentleman of leisure with an annual income of £8000. Vivian was educated at Harrow, showing an aptitude for maths and languages. In 1905 he indulged his passion for mechanical engineering by becoming a 'privileged apprentice' at the London and North Western Railway (LNWR) works in Crewe. He became interested in aviation and constructed a large model glider at Bodfari. In 1909 he rented shed No 18 at Brooklands and along with two companions went into business servicing and driving racing cars, as well as learning the rudiments of flying.

His first aeroplane was an Antoinette monoplane bought as a present by his exceedingly wealthy Uncle Tom. He did not find this underpowered machine very satisfactory and persuaded his generous uncle to replace it with a 25 hp (18 kW) Blériot at a cost of £1100.

On the untimely death of his father in 1910, Vivian returned home to North Wales in 1911. In February he bought a 50 hp (37 kW) Blériot XI and had gained more hours in the air from land he had acquired near Rhyl and renamed the Voryd or Foryd Aerodrome. He later wrote:

---

6   Ibid, p24
7   *Irish Times*, 18 October 1912

A portrait of Vivian Hewitt. *(Author's Collection)*

Vivian Hewitt's Blériot being towed by his powerful car. *(Author's Collection)*

"After spending a few days in London and having obtained most of the spares which I needed, I was thinking of returning to North Wales when, one morning, my mechanic came rushing into my room at the at the hotel where we were staying and, handing me a paper, said: 'Read that, Guvnor.' I did so. It stated that a man named Leslie Allen, who had been flying at Hendon for a short time, had started to fly to Ireland and was following the LNWR line with the object of reaching Holyhead and then crossing the Irish Sea. It was a terrible shock to me. I had been exhibition flying in North Wales ever since I left Brooklands in 1911, and there was my machine more or less dismantled at Rhyl where I had my headquarters. I had set my heart so much in wishing to be the first to fly the Irish Sea successfully, and here it was being taken out of my hands.

I remember saying to my mechanic that Leslie Allen would be across long before we could get back to Rhyl and have the machine re-assembled and in the air. The only thing which I could do was to complete my purchases of spare parts and wait for news of Leslie Allen. The next morning in a late edition the papers stated that Leslie Allen had passed over Holyhead at 8.15 am heading out over the Irish Sea. We waited for news, and very soon placards were out stating 'Missing Airman.' Late that afternoon more placards were out, and the evening papers reported 'Airman lost in Irish Sea.'

I said to my mechanic: 'Syd [Wingfield], come on, let's get back to Rhyl. I am afraid Leslie Allen has come down in the sea and I want to make the flight before someone else does it.' All that night we raced back on my Targ'u Floria Bianchi racing car which was fitted with powerful Rushmore headlamps. We arrived at Rhyl early the next morning and, with the help of my second mechanic, started assembling my Blériot monoplane".[8]

8  *Modest Millionaire*, p64–65

Having flown to Anglesey from Rhyl on 21 April, he was held up for several days at Holyhead by fog and gales "blowing at about 35 miles an hour in the wrong direction."[9] His experience thus far was described as follows and is a testament to the undoubted courage of these pioneer airmen flying into the unknown:

"I started from Rhyl at 5 am on Sunday morning and flew over the sea in the direction of Holyhead. After rounding the Great Orme at Llandudno I made for a point of land running out to sea. I could see Holyhead Harbour by this time, but the wind started blowing half a gale and I found it impossible to get there. I was up at an enormous height [5000 feet] and could distinctly see over Snowdon. The wind blew me right down the coast and I had to put the nose of my machine down and let my engine out, otherwise I should have been blown out to sea. I eventually landed at a place called Plas, in Anglesey at 6.20 am. I felt very sick, as I had been tossed about all over the place. The machine was roped down and next day I started for Holyhead at 9.30 am and landed in Lord Sheffield's grounds 20 minutes later."[10]

At Holyhead he was given a chart and a life-belt by Captain Clay, the ex-Commodore of the LNWR mail packet fleet, who also advised him on the best course to fly. The weather having relented, he set off across the Irish Sea and landed in Phoenix Park, Dublin, near the Hibernian Monument after a flight of 1 hour and 15 minutes. He was met by hearty cheers from the boys of the Royal Hibernian Military School, who, alerted by the noise of the approaching aeroplane had rushed out to greet him. He gave his thoughts on his flight to the press:

"I started at 10.30 on Friday morning. There was a good deal of wind and a lot of haze. I lost sight of land after about 10 minutes and 5 minutes later I sighted the

Ready to depart from Rhyl for Holyhead prior to crossing to Ireland. (Author's Collection)

9   *Flight*, 4 May 1912
10  Ibid

Hewitt's Blériot in Phoenix Park. *(Royal Irish Automobile Club)*

mail packet coming from Kingstown. I passed right over her from stem to stern and lost her smoke about three minutes after in the haze. Although all the boats had been informed and the mail packet was looking out for me, they never saw a thing, showing what a great height I was. After leaving the packet, I saw no more for 50 minutes and steered by the sun whenever I could. I ran into dense banks of fog and at times could not see the wing tips. Earlier on I had noticed the angle of the shadow of the sun on my wings. When I got out of the fog I adjusted the course of the plane so that the sun shadow fell approximately the same as before. I then saw the Wicklow Mountains and passed over Kingstown Harbour very high up. I passed over Dublin about 2000 feet up and when planing down experienced the worst air-currents that I have ever come across. I was all but upset twice, over Trinity College the machine was nearly turned upside down on me and dropped 500 feet, then crossing Guinness's Brewery I hit a pocket which was the worst I have ever met and I thought my flight was going to finish in the Liffey. I managed to land safely in the 15 acres in Phoenix Park and was treated very kindly by everyone."[11]

Vivian Hewitt portrayed in *Flight* magazine. *(Flight)*

A reporter from the Dublin *Evening Herald* interviewed Hewitt has left this very useful description of him:

"The aviator was partaking of light refreshments when he very kindly related his experiences. But twenty-four years of age, of medium height and slight build, fair complexion and clean

**FLIGHT PIONEERS.**

MR. VIVIAN HEWITT.
Who, on Friday, April 26th, flew over the Irish Sea from Holyhead to Dublin on his 50-h.p. Gnome-engined Blériot in 1 hr. 16 mins.

11 Ibid

shaven, his appearance struck one at once as boyish. Still retaining his motor scarf round his neck, he bore no traces of the recent strain through which he had come and told the story of his voyage across the channel in a simple, direct way."[12]

Another journalist, from *The Motor News*, took the opportunity to make some highly critical remarks concerning the Aero Club of Ireland:

"If the club had been in touch with aviation, Mr Hewitt would doubtless have informed the secretary of his project and then arrangements could have been made for the hospitable entertainment of the successful aviator. The club's lack of knowledge of aviation, however, is only exceeded by its want of energy. To all intents and purposes, it is comatose."[13]

The distances covered by Corbett Wilson and Hewitt were roughly the same and the aircraft similar, so he must have experienced a headwind or Hewitt a tailwind. Interviewed by the press, Hewitt expressed the view that Allen had been insufficiently experienced as a pilot for a flight across the open sea of such difficulty. It was contended by some, who were unaware of Corbett Wilson's flight just a few days earlier, that Hewitt was the first to make the crossing, others stated that his flight was a more difficult and dangerous feat than Corbett Wilson's. In any case he became a minor celebrity for a time, carrying out speaking engagements around the country accompanied by his parrot, which apparently had its own First Class seat when travelling by train. It is of interest to note that, oddly enough, Hewitt's aeroplane was returned home from Ireland in the same scenery box that

12  *Modest Millionaire*, p72–3
13  Ibid, p75

had just previously taken Robert Loraine's effects over there in connection with the GB Shaw play *Man and Superman* in which he was appearing at the Gaiety Theatre, Dublin. He continued to give demonstration flights and in April 1914 it was reported that he took to the air from Rhyl in his re-built Blériot with a small black lamb as his passenger.[14]

During the Great War Hewitt joined the RNAS but was passed medically unfit for front line service. He was based instead at Farnborough and from 1915, in the USA

**FLYING.**

Mr. VIVIAN HEWITT
The well-kno*v*n Aviator will give Exhibitions of
**Fancy . Flying**
ON THE
Rock Park Hotel Grounds,
ON
Wednesday, August 5th, at 3 p.m.

Admission to the Ground or Rock Park, **1/-**; Motor Cars **2/6** and **1/-** each occupant.    ⦅. The Exhibition can only be seen from the Grounds, and not from the road sides.

An advert for one of Vivian Hewitt's flying displays. *(Author's Collection)*

testing new aircraft for the Glenn Curtiss Company, retaining the rank of captain. By all accounts he was a kind, gentle and generous man, though he was something of an eccentric, the owner of one of the biggest stamp and coin collections in the world, he also set up a bird sanctuary at Cemlyn on Anglesey which still exists today and is run by the North Wales Wildlife Trust. In July 1959 he took part in the *Daily Mail* air race from London to Paris, celebrating the 50th Anniversary of Blériot's crossing, travelling by hire-car from Marble Arch, Air France from London Airport to Orly and to the Arc de Triomphe in a car driven by a French racing driver.

## The 'Great' Race

Considerable public interest was inspired on 9 September 1912 with the Air Race from Leopardstown to the Balmoral Show Grounds in Belfast, organized by the Aero Club of Ireland. It was described as an 'Open Event' with the winner being the competitor who, on an aeroplane in flight, accomplished the distance between Dublin and Belfast and back in the shortest time. Landing en-route was allowed, while a wait of half-an-hour at the Belfast Control was mandatory, though any time on the ground over the stipulated 30 minutes would be counted as flying time. There were no entry fees and competitors had to complete the official entry form by 1 August. The committee did not promise to pay the expenses of entrants but hoped to give each competitor up to £40 if the net profit was sufficient. Further particulars were available on request from the Secretary, Aero Club of Ireland, 35 Dawson Street Dublin or the Secretary, Royal Aero Club, 166 Piccadilly, London W.

"There were 16 entries originally including four Blériot monoplanes flown by Messrs Gustav Hamel, Henry JD Astley, Robert B Slack, and Denys Corbett Wilson, two Bristol monoplanes flown by Messrs Desmond Arthur and Harry Busteed, a Bristol biplane in the hands of Mons Henri Jullerot, two of the little Caudron monoplanes

Valentine discussing the weather
with Harold Perrin, Secretary of the
Royal Aero Club, and Astley. *(Royal
Irish Automobile Club)*

Desmond Arthur (left) and the Chairman
of the Aero Club of Ireland, John
Dunville. *(Royal Irish Automobile Club)*

to be handled by Messrs William H Ewen and E Obre, Mr Sidney V Sippe's Hanriot monoplane, and Lieutenant JC Porte's Deperdussin from the Military trials, Mr James Valentine's old 50 hp Deperdussin, an Avro biplane flown by Mr HR Simms, the Vickers and Handley-Page monoplanes, and the Twining biplane."[15]

The Great Northern Railway planned to run a special fast express open saloon train to allow spectators to view the contest. It was also intended to lay on exhibition and passenger flights at Leopardstown. In the event, the race was ruined by the weather and resulted in most of the original entries deciding not to take part much to the chagrin of the large crowd, which had gathered in Belfast to welcome the aviators, and who had to go home disappointed after patiently waiting all day. *Flight* magazine continued:

"More fortunate were the spectators at Dublin, as they at least saw all the four competitors get away and also witnessed some exhibition flights by Henri Salmet from Phoenix Park. From early morning a continuous stream of people flocked out from Dublin to the Leopardstown racecourse, which had been selected as the starting place, and every vantage point in the vicinity had its quota of enthusiastic watchers. Soon after 11 am Mr Astley made a trial trip on his Blériot, and the other machines were brought out for engine testing, but in view of the strong westerly wind, the start was delayed for some time. At 1.30 pm a message came through from Belfast that the weather was bad, there being rain and fog. Soon after the

---

15   Ibid, 14 September 1912

The police guarding Valentine's machine at Leopardstown. *(Royal Irish Automobile Club)*

proceedings were enlivened with a couple of circuits by Salmet, to be followed by a downpour of rain which drove everyone to shelter. This was succeeded by an unpleasant mist."

A decision had to be made or the day would soon be lost, though an amusing incident did lighten the mood:

"The afternoon was wearing on, and it became evident that it would be impossible for the competitors to return to Leopardstown that evening. It was, therefore, decided to finish the race, if it were found possible to hold it, at Belfast. During this period of waiting, a rabbit made its appearance, and was chased by the crowd into the hangar. It was finally caught by Valentine, and we suggested that he should take it with him in the race as a mascot, but he said it would in all probability die

Henry Astley stands in the cockpit of his Blériot. *(Royal Irish Automobile Club)*

Desmond Arthur in
the 'cabin' of his Bristol.
*(Royal Irish Automobile
Club)*

of fright at the noise of the Gnome engine.
The trembling quadruped was, therefore,
released by its captor."[16]

*Flight* takes up the story again:

"At 4.25 pm the weather was a little more
propitious, and Astley started on his Blériot
monoplane, followed by J Valentine on the
50 hp Deperdussin, Desmond Arthur on
the 70 hp Bristol, and Lieutenant Porte
on the 100 hp Deperdussin. Arthur failed
to get clear of the ground, and in landing
buckled one of his wheels. Lieutenant
Porte found the conditions much too trying, and after going three miles, returned
to Leopardstown. Astley and Valentine persevered through the vile weather, but
conditions got worse rather than better as they went on, while to add to their
difficulties daylight began to fail."[17]

*The Motor News* gave a more detailed description of Salmet's contribution to the day's
entertainment, giving flying exhibitions over Phoenix Park and Leopardstown:

"On Monday last, M Salmet, the famous French aviator, gave some excellent
demonstrations of flying in the Phoenix Park. He flew over from Leopardstown at

*Above:* Fortunately Thompson's
motor ambulance was not needed.
*(Royal Irish Automobile Club)*

*Right:* Lord and Lady Powerscourt
with Mr Delacombe. *(Royal Irish
Automobile Club)*

16  *The Motor News,* 14 September 1912
17  Ibid

about 9.30 am, and landed close to the Royal Hibernian Military School. In his flight from the scene of the start of the air race, he passed over a number of the suburbs, and was seen by great numbers of people, who were greatly interested in his performance. Soon after landing in the Park great numbers of people arrived at the Fifteen Acres in hopes of seeing some flying. Salmet, however, did not again mount his machine until 1.20 pm. He then proceeded to give the public an insight into trick flying, and delighted the onlookers with every description of aerial manoeuvre. He was in the air for about ten minutes. When he again reached terra firma the clever little pilot was heartily applauded, and was forced to indulge in much hand-shaking. After a short rest, the aviator again took to his favourite element, and sprinted down the Valley of the Liffey, returning again to his starting point in about ten minutes. Later on in the evening he again gave some demonstrations, this time before a large crowd, who called upon him for a speech. He responded in neatly turned phrases to the request, and thanked the crowd for their evident appreciation of his performances."[18]

Major Wellesley of the Irish Aero Club announces that Salmet will give an exhibition flight. *(Royal Irish Automobile Club)*

It also gave a full account of the somewhat truncated contributions of Arthur and Porte:

"The next man to start was Desmond Arthur, on the Bristol. He seemed nervous and excited. His engine was started up, but immediately showed signs of misfiring. Arthur ran her 'all out' for a few moments, and the missing then ceased. The signal was then given to let go, and the monoplane swung forward across the ground in the direction of the road facing the stand. But the machine refused to lift, owing to the bad condition of the engine, and the heavy loading of the machine. He therefore 'taxied' round to the right just in time to save himself from running into the crowd. The machine then careered onwards across the road running from the stands to the station, and the right wing struck one of the small flags with which the road was marked with absurd profusion. The near side tyre burst when it struck the 'kerb' of the road, and the machine came to rest a short distance from the Press tent. Arthur expressed the intention of making another start, and therefore had his machine wheeled back to his previous starting place. When, however, it was seen that the wing had been torn in striking the flag-post, he wisely determined not to make another attempt. Lieutenant Porte then prepared to follow the other two competitors. The 100 hp Anzani was started, and the machine made off in the direction of the hangar,

18 Ibid

which it cleared by about 40 feet. By this time the wind had risen considerably and was extremely gusty. The machine pitched and rolled in a most alarming manner, and the pilot had to indulge in terrific warps to counteract the powerful side gusts. He continued on as far as the Dublin side of Stillorgan, and was then forced to return. He landed with superb judgment, and stated that the control wheel had been almost wrenched out of his hands by the force of the gusts."[19]

The magazine also gave credit where it was due to a well-known motoring organisation:

"During the aviation meeting at Leopardstown the patrols of the AA did yeoman service in assisting the police to control the traffic between the city and the aerodrome. This was no light task, as there was an almost continuous procession of vehicles of all kinds on the road from fairly early in the morning until late at night."[20]

Of the few who started, only two, HJD Astley (1881–1912) (RAeC Certificate No 48, 24 January 1911), who alighted in a field a mile from the Drogheda Hotel in Co Louth and James Valentine, (1887–1917) (RAeC Certificate No 47, 17 January 1911), who got as far as Newry, Co Down, some 40 miles short of his destination. Astley had flown over Drogheda at 5.30 pm at high altitude. It is probable that he lost his bearings as, half-an-hour later, he was sighted over the River Boyne Viaduct, where, turning inland, he landed near Drogheda railway station.

---

19  Ibid
20  Ibid

Henry Astley takes off
from Leopardstown.
(*via Donal MacCarron*)

"I could not have gone ten minutes more. My stock of petrol was very low. A lot of kindly people turned up; the police took charge of the machine. You have to come to Ireland after all to meet real sportsmen."[21]

His engine had been giving Astley trouble for quite some time, so in view of the encroaching dusk he wisely decided to call it a day. Valentine described his flight to reporters as follows:

"I saw Mr Astley flying at about 4000 feet. From Skerries I gradually overtook him; the reason being that he was flying higher and encountering a stronger wind, and I soon passed underneath him. At Dunsany Point I turned towards the land, and had great difficulty in getting back to it. From there I could see that the Mourne Mountains were covered with rain and mist. I got on the Belfast course and made up my mind to weather the storm, if possible. I passed Dundalk safely but three or four miles on the other side my machine began to jump about and catch the wind badly. At one point I dropped from an altitude of about 1000 feet to about 200 feet in one swoop. I was turned around twice. I had to hand on to avoid falling out. It makes you dizzy sitting in that sort of position. My only consolation was the steady purr of the engine. In the deep valley at Newry, I saw at once it was hopeless. My machine had already survived more than I would have believed it was possible for it to endure."[22]

At 6.00 pm Valentine was observed some miles to the north over Dundalk at a height in excess of 2000 feet (609 m). Some 20 miles on (32 km), once more due to the failing light but also because of the severity of the gusting wind, he too decided to land. The spot he chose was a field in the townland of Ballymacdermott, belonging to the Widow Mallon, some two miles to the south of Newry. Valentine's arrival did not go unnoticed:

"It is said that an old man was engaged in a field adjacent when the machine landed. He had never, even in his dreams, heard of such a thing, and he at once concluded that some unearthly visitor had arrived. This idea was strengthened when he observed Mr Valentine in flying rig emerge from the machine. That the old man was a pious old man cannot be doubted, for he immediately began to appeal to all the saints he knew. On Mr Valentine approaching him, he was veritably tongue-tied and could only gesticulate."[23]

Leaving his aircraft in the charge of some agricultural labourers, Valentine walked into town where he was directed to the police barracks. District Inspector Irwin at once dispatched a posse of police to guard the machine. He stayed the night in the Victoria

21  *The Newry Reporter*, 10 September 1912
22  Ibid
23  Ibid

Hill Street, Newry
*(Image Courtesy of
the National Library of
Ireland)*

Hotel, having telephoned Dublin to arrange for his mechanics to come and dismantle the aeroplane. The next morning he returned to the field:

> "When I arrived there on Sunday morning, I found the machine surrounded by four high walls, over which nobody could see. They were formed of carts turned up, with canvas stretched between. Standing by were ten strong men, with sticks, to keep away small boys. They were charging threepence to each person who wished to go in. They let me in without paying. I suggested to the Widow Mallon that she should get something from the man who had started the show."[24]

He returned to Dublin by motor car, with the Deperdussin in tow. It was decided by the committee that the first prize of £300 should be divided between Valentine and Astley, plus £40 each for expenses, the £50 Shell Motor Spirit prize, plus £40 for expenses, went to Porte (1884–1919) (Aero Club de France Certificate No 548, 28 July 1911) and a special prize of £25, plus £40 for expenses, to Arthur.

Desmond Arthur (1884–1913) (RAeC Certificate No 233, 18 June 1912), who, it will be remembered, flew as a passenger with Grace at Leopardstown in 1910, lost his life in an air accident at Montrose in Scotland on 27 May 1913 in a BE2a, Serial Number 205, of No 2 Squadron RFC, where he was known for his adventurous nature, as well as his

---

24  Ibid

The No 2 Squadron BE2a No 205 in which Desmond Arthur lost his life. *(Author's Collection)*

unassuming manner and unfailing good spirit. He was the first Irish fatality in the air. A government inquiry was launched to investigate the circumstances surrounding the crash. The first inquiry found him responsible, but a later investigation exonerated Arthur. His name is most famously connected to sightings of a ghost believed to haunt the airfield site at the former RAF Montrose.

John Cyril Porte (1884–1919) was from Bandon in Co Cork, the son of Reverend Dr J Porte TCD. He had served as a submariner in the Royal Navy before contracting tuberculosis. Having learned to fly he became a civilian aircraft designer and test pilot, renowned for his work on flying boats. In 1914 he returned to uniform as a member of the RNAS, being given command of a training unit at Hendon Aerodrome in August 1914 followed by the naval air base at Felixstowe in September 1915. During his very distinguished naval service

Lieutenant John Cyril Porte. *(via Terry Mace)*

at Felixstowe, due to the reorganization of the different aerial services, Porte received various Naval, RNAS and RAF ranks, and served as a Lieutenant Commander, Wing Commander and Lieutenant Colonel. He retired with the rank of Colonel and died at the early age of 35 from a recurrence of tuberculosis. Walter Raleigh in his book, *The War in the Air*, was of the opinion that, "The shortest possible list of those who saved the country in its hour of need would have to include his name."

Henri Salmet with
his Blériot. *(Author's
Collection)*

## Henri Salmet

The next airman to give a display in Ireland followed very shortly afterwards on 11 September when Henri Salmet appeared at the first annual show to be held in Lurgan, a small town in Co Armagh 25 miles (40 km) from Belfast. Salmet was born on 22 July 1878 in Paris. In early 1911, he was in the employ of the Blériot Flying School at Hendon and was taught to fly by its Chief Flying Instructor, Pierre Prier. On 27 June 1911, he was awarded Aviator's Certificate No 99 by the Royal Aero Club. Later in 1911, he succeeded Prier as CFI. On 29 November 1911, he had broken the British altitude record in a flight to 8,070 feet (2,460 m). On 7 March 1912, in a Blériot XI, he attempted to break the record for the shortest time for a non-stop flight from London (Hendon) to Paris (Issy-les-Moulineaux) previously set by Pierre Prier on 13 April 1911. Salmet's time was three hours sixteen minutes, and that was duly reported in the press. However, Salmet later confessed that he had landed in France en route to Paris to locate his bearings, so the existing record was not broken. It would appear that he also instructed at the Blériot school at Pau, as he is mentioned as Deny Corbett Wilson's instructor.[25]

In July and August 1912, Salmet was one of the airmen who took part in the 'Wake Up England' aviation tour sponsored by the *Daily Mail*, the purpose of which was to promote public interest in aviation, visiting 121 towns, many of which were holiday resorts. The

Henri Salmet at Lurgan
as part of the 'Wake
Up England' aviation
tour sponsored by the
*Daily Mail. (Ernie Cromie
Collection)*

25  *Letters from an Early Bird*, p7

## AVIATION AT LURGAN.

SALMET, THE AVIATOR, GIVES A GREAT DISPLAY AT THE TOWN'S FIRST SHOW.

Salmet at Lurgan.
From the *Belfast Evening Telegraph*.
(*Central Newspaper Library, Belfast*)

display in Lurgan was held in the Public Park, under the auspices of the Agricultural and Recreation Association. The *Belfast Evening Telegraph* of 12 September had a spread of photographs showing, "The crowd inspecting the Blériot monoplane prior to the start: while others seek a vantage point to witness the display; Salmet in flight; and his arrival on terra firma." An accompanying article gives a flavour of the experience:

> "The large crowds had the good fortune to witness the most successful flights that have yet been made by an aviator in the North of Ireland. The intrepid airman, who has a most unassuming personality, made a couple of brilliant flights during the evening, and displayed to a remarkable degree the capabilities of the Blériot of which he had command, even under conditions not altogether too favourable in some respects, especially as regards the spectatorate, which over-ran the course and hampered to some extent the movements of the flying man in preparing for his descents. An official on horseback and other representatives of the association kept an open ground for the starting of the flight, which took place in moderate wind and in bright sunshine.
>
> Salmet went off like a bird – making a magnificent ascent, amid a tumult of cheering and for well over ten minutes he circuited and manoeuvred the machine, over which he had the most thorough command. On his successful descent within

Crowds gather around Salmet's plane at Lurgan. *(Central Newspaper Library, Belfast)*

the judging enclosure, after a clever volplaning movement, he was greeted with a salvo of cheers. He executed a series of clever manoeuvres on both occasions and was enthusiastically cheered for his brilliant display. He careered for some distance over the town, and after making several circuits descended with another splendid volplane. He displayed splendid judgement and precision of movement, and the entire display afforded intense delight to the great throng of the public assembled, many being ladies, and a great number having come from considerable distance. The luncheon and general catering arrangements at the show were most successfully carried out by the Bloomfield Bakery Ltd, under the direct supervision of Mr H M'Millan jun."[26]

## Two Aviation Meetings followed by tragedy in Belfast

In an effort to assuage the keen disappointment felt in Belfast over the non-arrival of any competitors in the Air Race, Harry Ferguson made representations to his fellow members of the Irish Aero Club. The result was that an Aviation Meeting, the first to be staged in Belfast, was arranged for Saturday, 14 September at Balmoral Show Grounds, the venue of agricultural shows since 1896. It was decided that three airmen would take part, Henry Astley and James Valentine, from the original list of race competitors, and Henri Salmet. It would appear that Salmet was a late addition to the bill as a contemporary advertisement in

26 *Belfast Evening Telegraph*, 12 September 1912

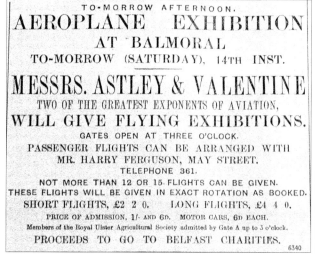

the *Belfast News Letter* on 13 September stated that an aeroplane exhibition would be held with flying by "Two of the Greatest Exponents of Aviation", Messrs Astley and Valentine. The gates would open at 3.00 pm and passenger flights could be arranged with:

> "Mr Harry Ferguson, May Street, Telephone 361. Not more than 12 or 15 flights can be given. These flights will be given in exact rotation as booked. Short Flights £2.2.0. Long Flights, £4.4.0. Price of Admission 1/- and 6d. Motor Cars 6d each. Members of the Royal Agricultural Society admitted by Gate A up to 3 o'clock. Proceeds go to Belfast Charities."[27]

The event was a considerable success, with all of the pilots giving good performances. Salmet added a flight over the Oval, the football ground of Glentoran FC in East Belfast, as a special gesture to the spectators. A display at the Oval had been cancelled owing to the unsuitability of the venue for take-off and landing.

*Above left:* An advert in the *Belfast News Letter* of 13 September 1912. *(Central Newspaper Library, Belfast)*

*Above (l-r):* Valentine, Salmet and Astley. *(Royal Irish Automobile Club)*

Salmet prepares for take-off. *(Royal Irish Automobile Club)*

27  *Belfast News Letter,* 13 September 1912

A couple of days later the Manager for Astley and Valentine, Harry Delacombe, wrote to the Lord Mayor of Belfast, RJ McMordie:

"Midland Station Hotel, Belfast. 18th September, 1912.

My Lord Mayor,

I am desired by Messrs Astley and Valentine to forward you herewith cheque value £161 5s 6d, this amount being the balance the gate receipts from the flying display at Balmoral show grounds on Saturday last after paying for hire of ground, wages, advertisements, and insurance. It is to be regretted that such a great number of people viewed the flights from outside the ground, even the noble cause of charity failing to appeal to their natures to induce them to part with the small sum of sixpence, to gain admittance to the enclosure, otherwise this cheque would doubtless have been for a larger sum. Whilst leaving the distribution of this money entirely to your discretion, Messrs Astley and Valentine express, the hope that the police orphanage and the Belfast hospitals may be given primary consideration – your obedient servant,

H Delacombe, Manager for Messrs Astley and Valentine."[28]

---

28  *Birth of Aviation in Northern Ireland*, p15

Astley sets out on his last flight. *(Royal Irish Automobile Club)*

It would appear therefore that the general desire to obtain something for nothing is by no means a modern phenomenon but at least the pilots and their manager were capable of a degree of altruism.

Tragedy was to follow, building upon the success of the first meeting, Astley and Valentine returned to Belfast a week later. On 21 September Henry Astley was killed while flying at Balmoral in front of a huge crowd, which was estimated to be between 10,000 and 12,000. A contemporary report stated:

"Mr Valentine was first up and gave a ten minutes' exhibition on his Deperdussin, after which Mr Astley ascended, but with no definite intention as to what form his flying would take. Just before starring for the flight Mr Astley was asked about the weather conditions, and his reply was, 'All right. Just enough wind to make it amusing.'

In endeavouring to keep within the limits of the oval shaped ground Mr Astley made some sharp turns, and in one of them apparently the machine side-slipped. The pilot evidently realized that a fall was bound to come, and set to work to keep the machine clear of the mass of spectators. At the Lisburn Road corner of the unreserved area he took a desperate chance in order to avoid injuring them, and 'banked over' his machine until the wings were almost at right angles to the earth. This he succeeded in doing, and the monoplane crashed down inside the track.

Unfortunately this brave and successful attempt to save the people massed outside the track cost Mr Astley his life. Mr Astley received such injuries to the head through being pitched violently forward from his seat that he died two hours later in the Royal Victoria Hospital, despite the endeavours of Professor Sinclair, the eminent surgeon, who happened to witness the fall. Professor Sinclair, who had been most assiduous in his attention to Astley in the hangar, accompanied him to the Royal Victoria Hospital.

It was seen at a glance that an operation was the man's only possible chance, and it was entered upon by Professor Sinclair and Dr Millar, the house surgeon, but death claimed the patient before it could be completed.[29]

The Showgrounds at Balmoral were narrow and really quite unsuitable for use as an airfield and flying display venue. The spectators' enclosures encircled the area and added to the difficulties Astley faced in trying to display his aeroplane within a confined area and give the spectators an equally good view. To this end he attempted to fly his 2-seater 70 hp (52 kW) Blériot inside the perimeter within the limits of the enclosures at a speed of about 60 mph (96.5 kmh). He therefore had to turn very steeply and it is probable that he failed to pull back sufficiently on the stick whilst steeply banked, thus side-slipping into the ground from a height of about 40 feet (25 m). He was not wearing a flying helmet, which it was believed might have saved his life. Astley was 31 years old and was the 21st British aviator to die in a flying accident and the first fatality in Ireland.

Harry Ferguson was among the many spectators who had a very narrow escape, it was reported that as Astley's aeroplane fell to earth, one of its wings brushed past Ferguson:

> "…coming down with a great velocity, actually flicking the hair of his head. He had to duck his head suddenly, getting out of the way not a moment too soon."[30]

29  *The Motor News,* 28 September 1912
30  *Belfast Evening Telegraph,* 21 September 1912

The wreckage of Henry Astley's aeroplane after his crash at Balmoral. *(Ulster Aviation Society)*

The *Northern Whig* reported on the aftermath:

"Shortly after the tragic occurrence an official informed the anxious spectators that Mr Valentine did not feel equal to making any further flights, as his close personal friend Mr Astley was then lying between life and death. The intelligence was received in sympathetic silence, and the crowd dispersed sadly, grieved and awed by the tragic ending to the proceedings."[31]

Henry Astley was a very wealthy young man, who, like many others of his ilk and era, craved the excitement and speed of fast cars. He was regarded as a capable and enthusiastic airman and had also served as a lieutenant in the 3rd Dragoon Guards. In 1909, he had been disinherited for a year after marrying the "very pretty and charming" Mary Ruth Kinder, a sometime Philadelphia telephone operator, who, unable to make her mark as an actress in America, had come to England in search of fame and fortune. She was at Hendon Aerodrome on the afternoon of Astley's crash, watching the flying. The grim news of the accident took some time to reach London, on hearing of her husband's death by means of a telegram sent by Valentine, she at once left for Belfast, accompanied by Astley's mother. At the inquest on Monday, 23 September a verdict of accidental death was returned. The *King's County Chronicle* reported,

Astley with his wife at Hendon. *(Author's Collection)*

"The funeral of Mr HJD Astley took place on Thursday 26th September at Ellesborough, Buckinghamshire. Thousands of citizens had marched in the procession from the Royal Victoria Hospital to the cross-channel steamer, and the Corporation of Belfast was officially represented. The mourners included Lady Florence Astley, Colonel the Hon Claud Willoughby MP, Mrs Astley (widow), Miss Astley (sister) and Mr R Astley, and among those present were the two airmen Mr Hamel and Mr Valentine."[32]

The Royal Aero Club carried out an investigation of the circumstances of the crash, coming to the following conclusion:

"Mr Henry J Delaval Astley was an experienced aviator, having made a large number of flights both in Great Britain and abroad … The Committee is of the opinion that the accident was entirely due to an attempt to make a very sharp turn at too low an altitude. At the last moment, the aviator made this attempt in order to avoid the spectators. Recommendation:- The Committee is of opinion that the ground

31  *Northern Whig,* 23 September 1912
32  *King's County Chronicle,* 3 October 1912

in question was unsuitable for the sort of exhibition flights which Mr Astley was attempting. It was too narrow for an aviator to attempt sharp turns at a low altitude and between spectators on either side of the ground. The inevitable danger from this condition of affairs should be made known to promoters and aviators."[33]

The *Northern Whig's* regular columnist, the 'Old Fogey' added a thoughtful piece on the wisdom of flying displays which may still be said to be apposite and relevant:

"The dominant feeling among the crowd who witnessed Saturday's accident seemed to be that life is too precious to be lavished unnecessarily in this campaign for the conquest of the air. These volplane swoops and 'banked turns' around a crowded aerodrome undoubtedly are more perilous to both the man above and the crowd below than a straightaway flight, with the wide circling turns which involve little or no 'banking'. Salmet is an adept in this art of 'trick-flying', as it may be called, but it is not given to every flying man to execute tricks with the same certainty and the same facility as the Frenchman does. The crowd likes to have its nerves thrilled by an eagle-like 'stoop' or a 'bank' which turns the airship on its heel like a racing yacht. But is it worth the risk? Such 'hanky panky' is really not necessary for any useful purpose to which flying can be applied – no more necessary than the tricks of the wheel acrobat of the stage are to the path rider or the soldier cyclist. It seemed fairly evident to everyone who witnessed the terrible disaster of Saturday that the theatrical side of the flying art was really responsible for the tragedy. And few people would care to purchase an extra thrill of excitement again at the risk of a repetition of the thrill of horror which Saturday's climax caused. Unless an undertaking be given that 'trick flying' will not be attempted many Belfast people will be shy of going again to an aviation exhibition. There would be in it too strong a suggestion of the circus of ancient Rome. One does not like to hear in fancy the airmen acknowledging his greeting with the words 'Morituri te salutaut.'"[34]

## The Irish Sea crossed again

The *Irish Independent* reported on Tuesday, 24 September that Denys Corbett Wilson had made a second crossing on 21 September, landing at Gorey in Co Wexford. It would appear that he had very favourable winds as it is reported that he covered 55 miles (88 km) in 45 minutes, averaging over 70 mph (112 kph). He had set off from Farnborough in Hampshire on 20th and flew some 220 miles (352 km) to Fishguard at an average speed of 80 mph (128 kph). The next day he crossed over from Fishguard to Rosslare and thence on to Gorey. On 22 September he arrived at Darver House, landing at 5.15 pm, where the now familiar throb of his motor was heard approaching. He made a successful descent amid the plaudits of a large gathering of country folk. He was next reported in the edition dated

33  *Flight,* 21 December 1912
34  *Northern Whig,* 23 September 1912

Denys Corbett Wilson prepares for flight. (*via Donal MacCarron*)

One of Denys Corbett Wilson's mechanics working on the machine. (*via Donal MacCarron*)

10 October flying from Kilkenny to Clonmel on Wednesday 9th, 30 odd miles (48 km) in 30 minutes and finally on 28 October it was noted that he attended the opening meet of the Kilkenny Hounds with Mrs Wilson.[35]

## James Valentine on tour

Following the tragic conclusion of the event in Belfast, James 'Jimmy' Valentine remained in Ireland with his Deperdussin Type B monoplane. This was the first product of the Société Pour les Appareils Deperdussin to

claim widespread attention when it appeared in 1911 and became available in single and twin-seat configurations. The airframe was constructed from ash and spruce, covered with aluminium (the engine cowling), plywood (around the cockpit) and oiled cotton (the rest of the fuselage, wings and tail). Valentine was born in Lambeth in South London on 22 August 1887, the son of James and Fanny Valentine. His father was the Managing Director of the Northern Insurance Company. Valentine had gained his RAeC certificate early in 1911 at Brooklands Aerodrome on an Empress-Macfie biplane. In June 1911 he was the only British aviator to compete in the 'Circuit of Europe' race, flying in France, Belgium and Holland in a Deperdussin, before crossing the Channel. He was respectably placed when engine trouble

35 *Irish Independent,* 24 September,/10, 28 October 1912

James Valentine
(left) 'transmitting
a wireless message'.
*(via Terry Mace)*

forced him to quit the race without crossing back to France. The following month, again
flying a Deperdussin, he was one of four airmen to complete the 'Circuit of Britain' race.
This was a testing event covering over 1000 miles (1600 km) in five days for a first prize of
£10,000. Another of the competitors was Henry Astley. Valentine finished the course, albeit
in second to last place. He completed the year by qualifying for the new advanced RAeC
Certificate in a Bristol monoplane, which he exhibited at the Paris Salon in December with
a daring flight over the city. He was accorded a very high accolade in a review of the year:

> "The name of James Valentine stands out before all others in British aviation. For a
> newcomer to flying the feats that he performed were prodigious, and his gameness
> in the face of the most disheartening adversity and his irrepressible good humour
> and sportsmanship, entitle him to be acknowledged as the greatest British pilot of
> the year."[36]

He continued to impress the following year, competing in several meetings, including
the Aerial Derby of 81 miles (128 km) around London on 3 June 1912, flying a Bristol Prier
two-seat monoplane, followed a month later by a triple crossing of the English Channel in
his Deperdussin. He was therefore a pilot of considerable renown. His first appearance of
his Irish tour was on Saturday, 28 September 1912 at Powerscourt in Co Wicklow, some
20 miles (32 km) south of Dublin. A brief report appeared in the local press:

> "James Valentine was a guest of the 8th Viscount and Viscountess Powerscourt at
> Powerscourt Castle on Saturday 28th September. In gusty weather gave a 10 minute

36  *History of British Aviation*, p127

Mr JH Robertson at the wheel of the Ford, with Valentine's French mechanic, M Bosserdet outside Powerscourt House. *(Royal Irish Automobile Club)*

flying display for 300 tenants and servants, making four circuits of the immediate area at a height of up to 1000 feet, flying over the Sugarloaf Mountain, circling Enniskerry and the castle grounds."[37]

The aircraft had been towed to Powerscourt by a Ford 20 hp (15 kW) car, owned by Lord Farnham. After a brief visit to Paris, Valentine returned to Ireland on 6 October and proceeded by motor car 50 miles (80 km) west from Dublin to Mullingar in Co Westmeath, where on Tuesday 8th, he made a couple of exhibition flights from the Newbrook Racecourse, flying around the town and then over nearby Lough Owel. Despite that fact that this had been arranged at a few days' notice business in the town came practically to a standstill for several hours that afternoon. The event commenced with a talk from Harry Delacombe, who was accompanying Valentine as his "able and courteous"[38] manager:

Newbrook racecourse Mullingar as featured in an old postcard. *(Courtesy of Westmeath County Library and Archive Service)*

> "…described the various portions of the machine and its principles of operation, Mr Valentine getting into the seat and showing the operation of tail, motor etc, while the propeller, wings, other parts and their functions were fully explained."[39]

37  *Freeman's Journal,* 30 September 1912
38  *Westmeath Examiner,* 12 October 1912
39  Ibid

When the engine was set in motion and the propeller began to turn, despite Harry Delacombe's[40] words of caution, the reporter and many of the spectators were surprised by the ferocity of the wind thereby created and the effect this had on their hats and other items of clothing. Valentine's amiable and friendly demeanour was also appreciated by the crowd, many of whom had shaken him by the hand and wished him 'God speed'. A stretch of grass in front of the grandstand had been mowed short as if being prepared for a game of cricket, only a portion of which Valentine used before rising into the air. He made three circuits of the course before landing to explain that he was making 100 mph (160 kph) with the wind but only 15 mph (24 kph) against it. Undeterred, he took off again half an hour later:

> "On this occasion he took a decidedly westerly course and at a height of well over a thousand feet, he flew over the town of Mullingar and then proceeded over the Military Barracks, St Finian's College, and Tullaghan, and across Lough Owel and on to near Multyfarnham. While he was in the air the wind went directly south-easterly, and he had a good deal of trouble in making the racecourse once more. But when he got over the grandstand he suddenly steadied himself and made one of the finest and most striking bird-like descents ever seen, to the great delight of the waiting gathering, who warmly applauded the daring aviator."

An advert for Valentine's performance in Co Cavan. *(Author's Collection)*

He spent the evening in Mullingar at the Greville Arms Hotel telling his enthralled listeners that he flew at 2500 feet (762 m) over Lough Owel in strong and gusty wind, at 90 mph (144 kph) in one direction and an average of 13 mph (21 kph) in the other. He also discussed his plans for an extended tour of Ireland, covered no less than 14 locations, the desirability of providing aviators and their passengers with parachutes and expressed his deep sorrow at the death of Henry Astley. Next day, with the wings removed, the Deperdussin taken from Mr Maher's coach factory, where it had been stored and was towed around 40 miles (70 km) north to Cavan in Co Cavan. The local newspaper, The *Anglo-Celt* described Valentine's appearance in Co Cavan on 10 October with great enthusiasm:

40 According to Howard Pixton, Harry Delacombe (1873–1959) was "a very, very nice man – a friend of pilots, always interested in flying but never flying himself except as a passenger. He was also a great pianist and simply loved London." He had served in the RN but had been first refused membership of the Aero Club (from 1910 Royal Aero Club) on the grounds that as he was *The Times'* aeronautical correspondent from 1893, he was a professional rather than a gentleman. He attained the rank of Lieutenant Colonel during WW1 and, presumably having thus regained the status of gentleman, became a highly respected member of the Royal Aero Club.

## FLYING AT CAVAN – MR VALENTINE'S SPLENDID PERFORMANCE AT FARNHAM DEER PARK

"On Thursday Mr James Valentine, the celebrated aviator, gave an exhibition in Farnham Deer Park, which was placed at his disposal by Lord Farnham. Mr Valentine is one of the most intrepid and successful aviators of the day and he has certainly not lost anything in reputation by his exhibition at Farnham. The crowd – between 2000 and 3000 – were most enthusiastic, the majority withall being somewhat apprehensive lest some accident should occur, as in the case of poor Astley at Belfast. Mr Valentine, however, seems to be a thorough master of his machine, and his graceful assents and descents were the admiration of all. He is a young man – possibly not 30 years – well set-up, and good-looking – (the ladies say handsome). There is nothing of what our Yankee cousins would call 'swank' about him and he really seems more at home in the rather confined seat of his monoplane than on terra, firma He goes about his work in an easy and confident manner which becomes contagious, the spectators being imbued with the idea that they have come to witness a performance by a master of his art and so events proved.

The first flight started at 3.53 pm. For an hour before the monoplane was on view, the unique design of the now-famous Gnome engine attracting particular attention. This is a most marvellous piece of mechanism, in fact its invention has made flying possible. The many cylinders of the engine radiate like a star but the most extraordinary thing of all is that, unlike other engines, the cylinders revolve, and that, too, at a speed of 2000 revolutions per minute. To this is attached the propeller,

Farnham Gardens in Cavan town. The statue of Lord Farnham now stands in front of the County Library. *(Courtesy of Johnston Central Library, Cavan)*

both being in front of the machine. The body of the monoplane would remind one of an eight-oared out-rigger, de-rigged. There is a rudder and a tailpiece, which are operated by the feet of the aviator. Extending like the wings of a bird are the planes, which are controlled by the steering wheel, the entire mounted on pneumatic wheels. The machine is but a bare framework covered with canvas the various parts being connected to the operating levers by the slenderest wires – wires as fine as a pin, that one may truthfully say the aviator's life is dependent on a single thread. Mr Valentine's machine is entirely of French construction and his mechanician is a Frenchman. It is proof of the marvellous genius of what now-a-days is considered a decaying nation. Flying machines are all right to talk about but men of nerve are required to manipulate them. Mr Valentine has the requisite amount of ability, nerve and enthusiasm."

James Valentine.
*(via Terry Mace)*

"The monoplane was anchored beside the enclosed rails where the bulk of the spectators assembled, and, with wheels blocked, Mr Valentine got aboard to test the engine. It got going, and a first-class South American tornado could not have had a more surprising effect on the spectators behind. The force created by the propeller seemed as if it would tear the grass from its roots. All being right, the machine was taken down to the starting place. Mr Valentine got into the crib, the French mechanic gave the propeller a few spins, the four men holding the tailpiece let go, and off he went. He ran about 70 yards on the ground, and then gradually and most gracefully arose. For twelve minutes he circled the valley, at times waving his hand to the spectators when 400 to 500 feet in the air. Mr Valentine went through a series of bird-like evolutions, and descended like one alighting on a basket of eggs, his contact with the earth was so sensitive and gentle. After about ten minutes he again ascended, this time to soar somewhat. The start was again perfect and after again circling around he got up to an altitude of 900 or 1000 feet. During the flight he got into a flock of crows, much to their consternation. The birds appeared to have lost their bearings as Mr Valentine circled around them, over and above, much to the delight of the spectators. The descent was again perfect. The crowd were most enthusiastic all through.

After a short interval a third ascent was made, the intention being to descend in front of Farnham House, but after a short flight the petrol gave out and Mr Valentine was compelled to come to earth. This ended a most successful exhibition by a master of the art. In Cavan almost all the business houses were closed, a half holiday being observed. Those in attendance included people from the town, Belturbet, Granard, Cootehill, Clones, Enniskillen, Bailieboro', Virginia, Oldcastle, Ballyjamesduff, Killeshandra etc and a large number from the rural districts."[41]

The Mall Castlebar.
*(Castlebar Library and Maggie Blanck)*

The next stage of the journey was 110 miles (174 km) from one of the nine ancient counties of Ulster to the far west of Ireland. The monoplane was transported to Castlebar in Co Mayo from Cavan on a motor lorry. Valentine and Delacombe arrived by train later. Once more the local newspapers gave extensive coverage to Valentine's display at the Asylum Grounds on 17 October. It had been postponed for two days owing to very heavy rain but on the Thursday it was sunny with light winds. Once more Valentine performed two flights, with Harry Delacombe again giving a talk. The *Connaught Telegraph* praised the two men for their spirit of co-operation with the organizing committee and noted that a reduced fee had been applied to take account of the extra expenses incurred owing to the bad weather delay.

41 *The Anglo-Celt,* 12 October 1912

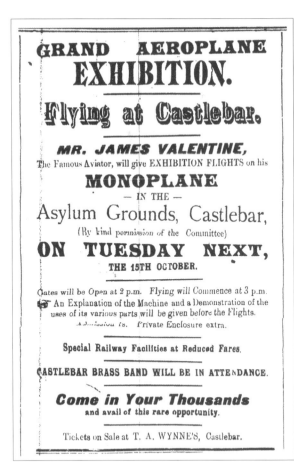

GRAND AEROPLANE
EXHIBITION.

Flying at Castlebar.

MR. JAMES VALENTINE,

The Famous Aviator, will give EXHIBITION FLIGHTS on his

MONOPLANE

— IN THE —

Asylum Grounds, Castlebar,

(By kind permission of the Committee)

ON TUESDAY NEXT,

THE 15TH OCTOBER.

Gates will be Open at 2 p.m.  Flying will Commence at 3 p.m.
An Explanation of the Machine and a Demonstration of the
uses of its various parts will be given before the Flights.
Admission 1s.  Private Enclosure extra.

Special Railway Facilities at Reduced Fares.

CASTLEBAR BRASS BAND WILL BE IN ATTENDANCE.

Come in Your Thousands
and avail of this rare opportunity.

Tickets on Sale at T. A. WYNNE'S, Castlebar.

An advert for Valentine's
visit to Castlebar.
*(Author's Collection)*

As for the event itself:

"When he was encircling the aerodrome the second time a most peculiar and unusual incident occurred; a large flock of seagulls, which for some time have been making their home at the Asylum buildings[42], flew around the machine, and their first inspection was evidently unfavourable, for they all flew away screaming."[43]

A good crowd had assembled to watch the spectacle and was entertained by the brass band of the Castlebar Total Abstinence Association. They were also given ample opportunity to inspect the machine at close quarters. The *Connaught Telegraph's* reporter took full advantage of this facility and gave his readers a very detailed description of what a flying machine actually looked like:

"To the casual observer, standing ten or twenty paces away, it looked quite insignificant, and it was only on close inspection that an idea of the elaborate mechanism could be had. At first glance it would give one the impression that it was a new kind of kite, the front portion was supported on an intricate carriage,

Castlebar Asylum
and grounds. *(Wynne
Collection via Tom
Kennedy)*

42  The Asylum was opened in 1865, renamed St Mary's Psychiatric Hospital in the 1950s and now houses the Galway-Mayo Institute of Technology (GMIT).

43  *Connaught Telegraph*, 19 October 1912

Tuam High Street.
*(Image Courtesy of the National Library of Ireland)*

composed of light wood and wire stays, there being a strong, expansive axle mounted on pneumatic, tired wheels, little stronger than bicycle wheels. Right over this carriage is placed the engine, steering mechanism and driving seat; the tonneau being constructed to hold only the aviator. Jutting out on either side of the pilot's chair are two expansive wings, parallelogram in shape and about 10 feet by 5 feet, composed of silk fabric, highly glazed, and almost resembling parchment, the superstructure being of some kind of special wood, and the whole kept in place by light wire cables, and controlled by the steering wheel, the manipulation of which showed them to be as sensitive as the pinions of a wild bird held in the hand. A long tail juts from the driver's seat to the back and ends in two peculiar tails; it is parallelogram in shape, tapering slightly towards the tails, which act as rudders, the hinder one being the smaller and perpendicular and the other larger and horizontal. The mechanism controlling both these rudders runs from the driving wheel in the centre of the tail. The rudders and tail are composed of the same material as the wings springing from each side of the engine and all are highly sensitive to the manipulations of the steering wheel."[44]

From Co Mayo Valentine headed 35 miles (56 km) south to Tuam in Co Galway, arriving on the afternoon of Friday 25th. The monoplane was reassembled on Saturday and public access was permitted. On the following day Harry Delacombe gave two lectures on the

44 Ibid

subject of "scientific research into air flying from the early ascent of the air balloon until the present day."[45] As was by now customary, before Valentine took to the air at Parkmore Race Course on Monday afternoon, Delacombe explained the technical details and operation of the aircraft. Two hopping exhibitions were followed by take-off and ascent to 500 feet (152 m) and a circuit of the grounds, avoiding some goal posts as he landed in the gathering gloom. The final stage of the tour was 138 miles (222 km) to the east, where three ascents were made at Curragh Grange, a Queen Anne style residence in four acres of gardens, designed by Richard Orpen, the residence of Captain and Mrs Harry Greer, on 6 November. The event had been advertised in the *Kildare Observer* of 2 November:

> "Admission 1/-, soldier in uniform and children 6d, 2/6 extra for the Reserved Enclosure, motor cars 2/-, horse vehicles 1/-. The event was under the patronage of General WP Campbell CB (GOC 5th Division). Afterwards a donation from the proceeds was made to the Drogheda Memorial Hospital at the Curragh."[46]

A modern aerial view of the Curragh. *(via Sergeant Wayne Fitzgerald)*

So ended Ireland's first aviation tour, which brought Valentine and his Deperdussin (and of course Harry Delacombe and his lectures) to eight venues. He was awarded the Silver Medal of the Royal Aero Club for his aviation achievements in 1912. Impressive though it was, it could have been even more so as *Flight* magazine had reported on 12 October as follows, "Mr Valentine now proposes to go on a tour round Ireland, giving exhibitions en remit wherever there are suitable grounds. It is probable the tour will include the following places:– Mullingar, Cavan, Enniskillen, Sligo, Castlebar, Galway, Limerick, Killarney, Cork, Waterford, Wexford and Drogheda."[47] It is possible that some organizers were put off the

45  *Tuam Herald,* 2 November 1912
46  *Kildare Observer,* 2 November 1912
47  *Flight,* 12 October 1912

idea following the tragic death of Henry Astley. The *King's County Chronicle* reported one instance of this, "At a meeting in Nenagh (in Co Tipperary and about 20 miles from Birr) in connection with the proposed aeroplane flights, Mr Waller, treasurer, said that only £13 had been secured. Mr Doran remarked that the tragic death of Mr Astley had thrown up the danger of the project. It was decided to return the subscriptions."[48] In 1913 Valentine married Louisa Eileen Knox in London, a fact which was noted in the *Anglo-Celt*, as follows, "Mr James Valentine, who gave the flying exhibition at Farnham, Co Cavan last autumn was married to Miss Eileen Knox, niece of the Earl of Lonsdale."[49] With the outbreak of the First World War Valentine joined the RFC in 1914. He was placed in charge of the aviation depot at Le Bourget in Paris. His driving skills received very favourable mention from Hugh Trenchard's assistant, Maurice Baring:

> "On 13th August 1915 Valentine drove me back from Paris in his racing Panhard. We left Paris at 4.15 and arrived at St Omer at 7.20. Valentine drove at terrific speed but with consummate skill. He would calculate accurately what a man in a cart about three-quarters of a mile ahead would be likely to want to do … And not give him time to do it."[50]

Valentine was later sent on special missions to Italy and Russia. By now a major, he was awarded the Russian Order of St George 4th Class, to add to his French Légion d'Honneur and the British DSO. He died in Kiev on 7 August 1917 due to illness and inadequate medical care.

---

48  *King's County Chronicle*, 2 October 1912
49  *The Anglo-Celt*, 21 June 1913
50  Flying Corps Headquarters 1914–1918, p104

Chapter 5

# Further Progress:
# 1913

## Lywood and Williams

IN FEBRUARY 1913 *FLIGHT* magazine recorded that Harry Ferguson's aircraft had taken to the air again but not flown by Ferguson himself:

> "Recently Mr Harry Ferguson's monoplane has been flying again at Magilligan. The pilot was Mr OG Lywood, who was making his first essay on a single-decker, his previous experience having been with a Bristol biplane. Although there was a wind of between 20 and 30 mph blowing and the circumstances were very unfavourable, Mr Lywood says that no machine could have been easier to manage. For over an hour Mr Lywood was making straights on the machine, rising to a height of 40 feet and landing by *vol plané*. He says that he cannot speak too highly of the design and construction of the Ferguson, which has stood two years' exposure to the weather."[1]

Second Lieutenant Oswyn George William Gifford Lywood (1895–1957) was just 18 years old and would not attain his RAeC Certificate until the following summer (No 600,

The Ferguson Mk 2 at Magilligan in November 1912. Ferguson is on the far right beside Lywood. *(Author's Collection)*

1  *Flight,* 8 February 1913

21 August 1913 in a Bristol Biplane at Brooklands). He would have a very distinguished career, commanding the British Expeditionary Force's first wireless telegraphy signals unit on the Western Front in the Great War and rising to the rank of Air Vice Marshal in the Second World War.

Sadly Lywood's very positive experience was not replicated by Ferguson's friend and colleague, Jack Williams, in April 1913. The local press reported that a hangar had been erected at Castleleavery, on the shore of Strangford Lough between Newtownards and Comber. It added that several short hops had been flown, possibly by Lywood and that Williams had taken the aeroplane out for a 'trial roll':

> "The engine was running sweetly, and Mr Williams travelled very fast over the sands, and everything seemed to be going extra well. On approaching the hangar, after a satisfactory trial, by some means the tail of the aeroplane touched the earth. This action caused the planes to elevate and, the contact giving the machine the necessary propulsion, up the aeroplane flew into the air to a height of possibly 50 feet, the engine meanwhile recording revolutions indicating a speed of over 60 miles an hour. If the machine went up quick, it came down still quicker, causing those who beheld the sight to hold their breaths, under the impression that Mr Williams must of necessity meet with fatal injuries.[2]

Fortunately Williams was not killed, though such was the force of the impact that his waist strap was broken in two. He was, however, knocked unconscious and given first aid by two doctors who had rushed to the scene. Later, while he was recuperating in the Ulster Hotel, it was decided that his helmet had saved him from greater injury. So ended the flying career of the Ferguson monoplane. Williams would serve with the RFC in the Great War.

## Ronald Whitehouse

There were no further performances until August 1913 when Ronald Whitehouse (1894–1979) (RAeC Certificate No 407, 21 January 1913) was engaged to fly his Handley Page Type E 50 hp (37 kW) monoplane at the Lurgan Agricultural Show. Whitehouse was from Sunderland and had become a staff pilot with Handley Page, as well as a test pilot and Chief Instructor at the Handley Page School at Hendon. He was mentioned in *Flight* many times during 1913; other venues on same tour as Lurgan included Leicester, Mansfield, Lincoln, Hull and Beverley. In Hull he had avoided prosecution by the Chief Constable of the East Riding for breach of the Lord's Day Observance Act, when the magistrates dismissed the summons on the grounds that they required further evidence to prove that the Act related to aviation exhibitions.[3] The Type E had first flown in 1911 and was a two-seat machine, with a fuselage covered in thin, varnished, mahogany ply sheet. The engine was enclosed within an aluminium cowling. The bleached cotton covering on the gracefully curved wing

---

2 *Newtownards Chronicle,* 5 April 1913
3 *Freeman's Journal,* 17 July 1913

Ronald Whitehouse
at Lurgan in his
Handley Page Type
E 50 hp monoplane,
*Yellow Peril*. *(Author's
Collection)*

and tail surfaces had been given a protective coating of cellulose, the distinctive colour of which led to the aeroplane's nickname *Yellow Peril*.

The display in the Public Park at Lurgan was something of an anticlimax, despite beautiful weather and a record attendance, as, owing to engine trouble, the only flight of the day was severely curtailed and the promised joy-rides at two guineas a time never materialized as the young pilot did not wish to expose passengers to any avoidable risk:

> "When the monoplane was brought into the enclosure the aviator tried the engine by a swift run the length of the ground. Then turning, he quickly covered half the distance of the enclosure and rose gracefully in mid-air. He cleared the big trees at the far end of the park and then circled to the left about 200 feet from the ground. Finding that the engine was still not working properly, Mr Whitehouse volplaned down into a big grass field a short distance outside the public park, and afterwards returned on foot to the show ground. He announced that it would be impossible to give a further exhibition and naturally the crowd were greatly disappointed."[4]

The public had to be content with examining or possibly sampling prize horses, donkeys, cattle, goats, sheep, pigs, poultry, pigeons, butter, eggs, flowers, fruit, vegetables and home

4  *Belfast Evening Telegraph*, 21 August 1913

Ronald Whitehouse
and the *Yellow
Peril. (Handley Page
Association)*

baking. Show jumping and driving competitions were also a feature, while entertainment
was provided by the band of the 5th Royal Irish Lancers. As was the case with several
other pilots, he had not flown across from Great Britain but had brought his aeroplane
over on the steamer. Indeed the Handley Page Association Archivist, Bryan Bowen, noted
that, given the problems with the Type E's engine, a cross-channel flight would have been
a risky proposition.[5] Whitehouse served in the Royal Naval Air Service during the Great
War. He was appointed a temporary Major in the RAF in September 1918. He remained in
the Service and attained the rank of Squadron Leader before retiring in 1931, having seen
duty in Egypt and Iraq. Finally it is of interest to note that Whitehouse was undoubtedly air-
minded from an early age. In 1910 he wrote to *Flight* magazine taking issue with a previous
correspondent who had cast aspersions on James Radley's flying skills.[6]

## Corbett Wilson

Early in 1913 it was reported in both the French and Swiss press that Corbett Wilson made
some "splendid flights" in France and Switzerland, notably one from Pau to Orthez and back,
a two-hour's long tour of the valley of the River Gave and across the Jura Alps from Dijon
to Lausanne. However, he did not ignore his countrymen in Ireland; the *Munster Express* of
Saturday, 19 July 1913 reported on a flight performed at the Waterford Agricultural Show
on 17 July, from St Patrick's Park.[7] On Wednesday 16th he flew over the short distance to
Waterford from Woodstown, the residence of Mr Barron, the President of the Society, with
two passengers. Later that morning the propeller of his 70 hp (52 kW) Blériot was damaged

5  Letter to the author dated January 2015
6  *Flight*, 3 September 1910
7  *Munster Express*, 19 July 1913

when it hit an obstruction on take-off. Neither the pilot nor his passenger, a journalist from Dublin, were hurt. A replacement part was ordered urgently by telegram from the Blériot Monoplane Company's London office at Hendon. It was conveyed by high-speed motor car to Paddington where the District Messenger Service courier just missed the Rosslare Express. He rushed to Euston and caught the Holyhead and North Wall Express. From Dublin he took the morning train to Waterford. Corbett Wilson's two French mechanics swiftly installed the propeller, so enabling a display to be flown that afternoon, accompanied Lieutenant Anthony Loftus Bryan, South Irish Horse, who was a neighbour in Kilkenny, before a huge crowd. Corbett Wilson took off from the show jumping arena, from which a couple of fences were removed and planks laid across the water jump:

*Below:* Denys Corbett Wilson and his mechanic. *(via Terry Mace)*

*Below right:* Denys Corbett Wilson in his favourite flying coat. *(Donal MacCarron)*

"The Blériot was splendidly handled by the skilful pilot, who made several graceful circles over the ground and once created a mild sensation by partially shutting off the engine and planing down to within about 70 feet of the ground, rising again to several hundred feet. Finally he steered a course over the city and, having returned, he circled the ground once more before he made a safe landing at the appointed spot, just outside the enclosure. When Mr Wilson walked into the enclosure he was seized by some enthusiastic onlookers and carried shoulder high around the ground, receiving a great ovation."[8]

8  *Irish Examiner*, 18 July 1913

On his way from Bournemouth to Ireland he had landed near Wells in Somerset, giving the local newspaper's reporter the opportunity to describe the garb of a 'flying man':

> "The aviator, who is a middle age gentleman, [Corbett Wilson was 31 years old] was dressed in a costume suitable for resisting the cold while flying. A thick woollen vest covered the waistcoat of his morning suit, and on top of this a short fur lined coat, whilst he wore a special head cap and thick gloves. The mechanic [Monsieur Potet] was dressed in yellow overalls."[9]

In August 1914 it was announced in the *London Gazette* that Corbett Wilson had been appointed to the Special Reserve of Officers in the RFC Military Wing as a 2nd Lieutenant, having resigned a previous commission in October 1913. His mishap with Robert Lorraine has already been described. It is also of interest to note that Corbett Wilson also served with the great British ace James McCudden, who at that time was a Sergeant Air Mechanic. When on leave in Paris in February 1915 he has lunch with James Valentine, with whom he had attended the flying school at Pau. Apparently he thought that Valentine was rather standing on his dignity as a Captain.[10]

Morane Parasol Serial No 3260 of No 3 Squadron. *(Donal MacCarron)*

Still with No 3 Squadron, on 10 May 1915 Corbett Wilson and his 18-year-old observer, 2nd Lieutenant Isaac Newton Woodiwiss, were on a reconnaissance mission in a Morane Parasol L No1872 when their aircraft was struck by an enemy shell. Both were reported to have been killed instantly. He is buried in the Cabaret-Rouge British Cemetery, Souchez, France. The high esteem in which Corbett Wilson was held may be judged from the following letters sent to his mother:

> "Dear Mrs Wilson,
> I am very sorry to have to write and tell you that your son, Corbett Wilson, is missing. He left on May 10th with an officer called Woodiwiss for a reconnaissance on a Parasol Morane, and has not returned, and on May 11th the Germans dropped a message from one of their aeroplanes to say that artillery had hit one of our machines and that the two officers were killed and were being buried in the cemetery East of Fournes in German lines. I fear this machine was the one your son was in, as it was about the correct time, and they called the machine a parasol aircraft. I must say that we all feel his loss terribly, even in this terrible war. He was one of the most gallant officers I have met, and one of the best. He did not know what fear was; he always did his work splendidly. He was very popular with all, and would have made

9 *Somerset and West of England Advertiser,* 4 July 1913
10 *Letters from an Early Bird,* p140

a name for himself. If I ever get the chance I will try and find the place at Fournes and will try and come and see you after the war.

Yours sincerely

Hugh M Trenchard[11] 1st Wing, Royal Flying Corps British Expeditionary Force"

"Dear Mrs Corbett-Wilson:

You will have heard by now of the sad death of your son. He was killed by a shell whilst doing a reconnaissance over Fournes. A German aviator dropped a message yesterday to say that he and his observer, Woodiwiss, were both killed instantly and were being buried at a cemetery at Fournes. When I advance I will try to locate the spot and mark it. I can't say how sorry I am to have lost your son. He was as gallant a fellow as I know, and he is much missed by us all. His kit has been sent to Cox & Co., Charing Cross, and an inventory by post. Allow me to offer you my sincerest sympathy,

Yours sincerely,

DS LEWIS (Major)"[12]

## The First Aerial Crossings to the North and the First Military Aircraft

### Harry Hawker

Harry Hawker.
(Author's Collection)

History was made in August 1913, when the great airman, Harry Hawker (1889–1921) (RAeC Certificate No 297, 17 September, 1912) and his mechanic Harry Kauper (1888–1942), became the first men to fly across the North Channel to Ulster. They were taking part in a multi-stage, 1540 mile (2478 km) Circuit of Britain flight for a prize of £5000 offered by the *Daily Mail*. Hawker's aircraft was a Sopwith HT (Hydro Tractor) 100 hp (74 kW) Biplane Seaplane. On 27 August he flew from Oban to Larne Harbour, where he refuelled before setting out for Dublin. Having taken off from Oban not long before 7.00 am, the machine was observed some 40 minutes later by the Ballycastle Coastguards flying over the calm sea between Fair Head and the Mull of Kintyre. The *Larne Weekly Telegraph* noted:

"Late on Tuesday evening [29th] a message was received at Larne Harbour by Mr Thomas Jack, managing director of the Shamrock Shipping Co, that Hawker would leave Oban the following morning and asking that petrol, oil, water and other necessaries should be taken out in a boat to meet him. As was only natural a number of people were early astir in Larne, this being the first visit

---

11 Colonel Trenchard (1873–1956) would rise to the rank of Marshal of the Royal Air Force and be raised in the peerage to a viscountcy. He would become known as the 'Father of the RAF'.

12 Ibid, p167–8

The Sopwith seaplane at Oban with Kauper (left) and Hawker (right). *(Author's Collection)*

of an air machine of any sort. It was 9.00 am before the first glimpse was obtained and this was signalled from the Stranraer steamer *Princess Maud* which was lying just outside the lough. The noise of the siren was quickly followed by the sirens and whistles of all the craft lying in the harbour; and in a couple of minutes the machine was plainly visible to all. At first it appeared like a big bird on the horizon but quickly its proportions grew and it became evident that Hawker intended to descend immediately. A beautiful descent was made opposite the lighthouse at the entrance to Larne Lough and, on its floats, the huge machine swiftly passed through the narrow waterway to where the pilot boat was stationed. With the greatest ease the airmen made fast to a buoy just off the south pier in the bay, in front of the Olderfleet Hotel, amidst the delighted cheers of hundreds of spectators."[13]

Harry Hawker alights on Larne Lough in 1913. *(Mid and East Antrim Borough Council)*

For the next hour or more the two aviators were hard at work rectifying a choked engine oil pipe and replacing the spark plugs. He refused the proffered alcoholic beverages, saying

13  *Larne Weekly Telegraph,* 30 August 1913

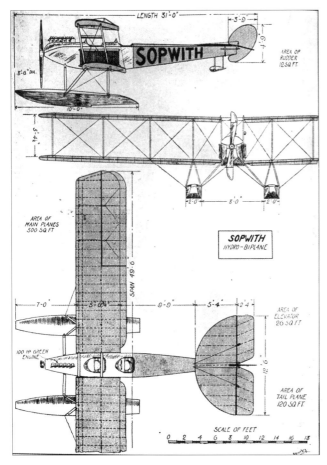

Plan of Hawker and
Kauper's Sopwith
'Hydro-Biplane'.
*(Author's Collection)*

that he was strictly TT but accepted a cigarette and some light refreshment. Just before 11.00 am Hawker indicated that he was ready to depart:

"In the meantime an immense crowd gathered on the pier head and on the various steamers to witness the novel sight, and everyone had a splendid view. Scores of small boats plied hither and thither, making a circuit of the plane, and hundreds availed themselves of this opportunity of seeing the novel craft at close quarters…. rousing cheers greeted the intrepid aviator as his machine sailed overhead out of the Lough."[14]

Further down the coast the aeroplane was observed over Whitehead crossing the mouth of Belfast Lough in the direction of Donaghadee. Spectators witnessed "the waterplane in full flight" from vantage points in Carrickfergus and Bangor. As it passed Ballywalter the lightship was heard firing a salute. By 12.15 pm Hawker was passing over Ardglass. Unfortunately mechanical problems induced a forced landing in the sea off the Irish coast at about 2.00 pm only 13 miles (20 km) from Dublin, in which the aeroplane was broken up, luckily without life-threatening injury to Hawker or Kauper. Having covered more than 1000 miles (1600 km) of the course, Hawker

14  Ibid

Harry Hawker in Larne Harbour.
*(Mid and East Antrim Borough Council)*

The wreck of Hawker's aeroplane being towed ashore. *(Author's Collection)*

was given a special prize of £1000. He would also be awarded the RAeC Silver Medal, with a Bronze Medal going to Kauper.

The two young men, along with another airman of the future, Harry Busteed, had travelled from their native Australia in 1911 to seek fame and fortune in the British aviation business. Both Hawker and Kauper found this with the Sopwith Company, as Chief Test Pilot and Works Manager respectively. Sadly Hawker was killed in a flying accident in 1921. Kauper eventually returned to Australia, contributing to the development of portable radios for the Flying Doctor Service.

## The Royal Flying Corps

It was also noted in the *Larne Weekly Telegraph* that on Wednesday, 27 August 1913:

> "The observer of the Royal Army Aero Corps [sic] who had visited Islandmagee to select ground for the descent of the Army biplanes at present in Scotland paid a visit to Mr Hawker and proffered the assistance of mechanics etc., but they were not found necessary."[15]

The first association between the Royal Flying Corps and Ireland was equally as historic as Hawker's flight. It occurred on 1 September 1913 at 1.50 pm when Captain George William Patrick Dawes landed on the beach at Newcastle, Co Down near the Slieve Donard Hotel. This was the first ever overseas deployment of the Royal Flying Corps (RFC). Five BE2a aircraft, serial numbers 217, 218, 225, 272 and 273, flown by Captains JWH Becke, CAH Longcroft and ACH McLean, Lieutenants FF Waldron and L Dawes and a single Maurice Farman Longhorn, No 207, piloted by Captain GWP Dawes, all of No 2 Squadron based at Montrose, flew from Scotland on their way to take part in large-scale Irish Command manoeuvres centred around Rathbane Camp near Limerick.

George Dawes was born in Dublin on 25 January 1881, while his mother, Pauline, was

15  Ibid

Officers of No 2 Squadron Royal Flying Corps (Military Wing), August 1913. *L–r:* Captain CAH Longcroft, Welsh Regiment; Captain GWP Dawes, Royal Berkshire Regiment; Major JWH Becke; Lieutenant FF Waldron, 19th Hussars; Lieutenant ACH McLean; Captain F StG Tucker and Lieutenant L Dawes, Middlesex Regiment. Behind them is one of the Squadron's BE2a biplanes. All of these aviators – apart from Captain Tucker – flew to Ireland on 1 September 1913. *(Museum of Army Flying)*

visiting her mother. His father was an ironmaster and the family home where he grew up was at Kenilworth in Warwickshire. George enlisted in the Royal West Surrey Regiment as a 'gentleman ranker' in 1900 and earned a battlefield commission in the South African War with the Royal Berkshire Regiment. A decade later, he was the first serving officer in the British Army to be awarded the Royal Aero Club Pilot's Certificate, flying a Humber Monoplane at Wolverhampton. He received Certificate No 17 on 26 July 1910 (the founder of the famous aero company AV Roe was No 18). In 1912 he joined the Military Wing of the Royal Flying Corps and was posted to No 2 Squadron at Farnborough.

In February 1913 the squadron moved to Montrose. Planning for the deployment to Ireland was started in March and letters were exchanged between the War Office, the Director of Military Training, the Officer Commanding the RFC at Farnborough, Lieutenant Colonel Frederick Sykes, the CO of No 2 Squadron, Major CJ Burke, Royal Irish Regiment (an Ulsterman from Co Armagh) and the GOC Irish Command. An estimate of costs was drawn up for the sum of £1115, to include transporting officers and men, mechanised transport (MT), hangars and spares from Montrose to Limerick and return; MT for use in Ireland; hire of camps and landing grounds; compensation for damage; field and travelling allowances.[16]

BE2a No 328 flies over Montrose in 1913. Maurice Farman Longhorn's 214 and 215 are to the right. *(JM Bruce GS Leslie Collection)*

---

16  Air1/802/204/4/1119 letter from 2 Sqn to OC Military Wing RFC dated 22 September 1913

Captain Dawes' Maurice Farman Longhorn and three of the five BE2a biplanes of No 2 Squadron RFC at Cults Farm, Castle Kennedy in August 1913. The flotation bags for the North Channel crossing referred to in the text are clearly visible on No 272. Some years ago Mr Donnie Nelson, a reporter with a Stranraer newspaper, was given a first-hand account of this scene by an elderly gentleman from the town, Mr William McConnell. As a child, Willie McConnell helped mark out the field to be used, with two of his mother's white table-cloths. He lived in an adjacent cottage and may well be the boy in the photograph. *(JM Bruce/GS Leslie Collection)*

The aircraft departed from Montrose on 27 August. Flotation bags were fitted to the underside of the wings of the aircraft at Cults Farm on the Earl of Stair's estate near Castle Kennedy, Wigtownshire, against the possibility of a ditching in the often choppy waters of the North Channel. These did nothing to improve the flying or handling qualities of the aeroplanes. Some degree of reassurance was provided by the presence of the super-dreadnought, HMS *Bellerophon* cruising in the vicinity of the route. It may be noted that the warship's name was a happy chance in the light of its future association with soldiers of the air – being the rider of Pegasus, the winged stallion of Greek mythology. The first to take off from Cults Farm was George Dawes in the Farman, followed by Waldron, Longcroft, Becke and Leonard Dawes. McLean did not leave with the others as he had a damaged propeller shaft which needed repairs, while Longcroft had to return with a loose float.

It had been George Dawes' task to travel by steamer to Larne the week before to scout out possible landing sites. The local press reported that he had selected a field on Islandmagee, near Larne as being "suitable in every way for the brief occupation of the airmen."[17] The town missed its chance to be part of this memorable event as:

> "The commercial instincts of the owner of the land obviated the acceptance of the officer's terms, which were said to have been fairly liberal."[18]

In the event Larne and Islandmagee missed out as the Belfast newspaper, the *Northern Whig* reported under the headline:

---

17  *Larne Weekly Telegraph*, 23 August 1913
18  Ibid

Captain Dawes, of the Army Flying Corps, who left Stranraer at 1.15 on Monday afternoon, landed on the beach at Newcastl[e]
Co. Down, at ten minutes to two. The above picture shows the machine, surrounded by a crowd of spectators. / Inset—Captain Daw[es]
in flight.

Photographs of
Captain Dawes stop at
Newcastle appeared
in the *Belfast Evening
Telegraph* the following
day, 2 September 1913.
*(Central Newspaper
Library, Belfast)*

### ARMY FLYING CORPS – CAPTAIN DAWES ALIGHTS AT NEWCASTLE

"He passed over the sea to opposite the centre of the town, where he turned and flew towards the sandy part of the beach near the Slieve Donard Hotel and had a most graceful descent. Captain Magill received the intrepid airman and ministered to his wants and also assisted in overhauling the machine. After replenishing the petrol tank, Captain Dawes set the propeller in motion at 2.50 pm and swept along the beach for a short distance in the direction of Dundrum and rose. Turning, he proceeded with his mechanic, Mr Traylor, who arrived on 30th of the month to inspect the beach for the purpose of alighting. He flew in a southerly direction, skirting the Mourne Mountains, flying at a height of about 1000 feet. A very large crowd, assembled on the beach, and numerous camera operators were busily engaged photographing the airman and his machine. The other aircraft [Becke, Waldron and L Dawes] did not stop. They passed Newcastle at 1.45 pm, 3.32 pm and 3.45 pm, the last machine especially flying at a very high altitude."[19]

A hand drawn sketch map prepared by the Squadron on 20 August identified landing grounds en-route at Portadown and the Curragh.[20] It would appear therefore that George Dawes selected the beach at Newcastle on his own initiative. One of the BE2s (possibly No 217, Becke) flew over Dublin where it was observed by many of those taking the air

19  *The Northern Whig*, 2 September 1913
20  Air1/802/204/4/1119

in Phoenix Park, while No 273 flown by Waldron landed at the Curragh[21] to refuel, having first alighted at Donadea Castle in northwest Kildare. The *Kildare Observer* noted:

> "The military men caused quite a sensation on Monday when passing over Co Kildare in a southerly direction. They were the first, as far as we know, to pass over the county and, of course, many of the residents had never seen an aeroplane before."[22]

And added:

A BE2a in flight.
*(No 2 Squadron Archive)*

> "Lieutenant Waldron from a considerable height communicated a request by megaphone to Mr Battersby who was on his way to Kilcock station and asked as to where he could be supplied petrol."[23]

At Dondea Miss Caroline Aylmer's[24] manager, Mr Corbally, supplied the Waldron with eight gallons of petrol. Word spread throughout Donadea, Stapleston and Rathcoffey of the aerial visitor and soon a crowd had collected on the Donadea Castle grounds and "immensely enjoyed the rare spectacle"[25], it being the first time ever they had come close to an aircraft. Francis Fitzgerald Waldron known to his friends as 'Ferdy' was no stranger to Co Kildare, having been born at Melitta Lodge on the Curragh, only son of Brigadier-General Francis Waldron.

Meanwhile, Lieutenant Dawes in the BE2a No 225 broke his journey at the Royal Field Artillery Barracks in Dundalk. The *Dundalk Examiner* reported on the sensation that his arrival caused in the town:

> "On Monday evening about 4 o'clock the machine was first sighted in the direction of Carlingford when it appeared as a mere

Dundalk Artillery Barracks.
*(Dundalk Library)*

21  The Curragh has been associated with military activity for centuries. There is a description of Kildare dated 1683 which refers to the Curragh and points out that "upon any general meeting or rendezvous of the Army or militia this is the place". The extensive Curragh plains have afforded manoeuvre room for infantry, cavalry and artillery units over hundreds of years. However, despite this close military association the first permanent camp was not established on the Curragh until 1855. It was also known as the "finest racing ground within the Empire, a gently undulating plain covered with a fine, velvety, elastic sward, perpetually green."

22  *Kildare Observer,* September 1913

23  Ibid

24  She was the last of the Aylmers, who had owned the demesne since 1597.

25  *Kildare Observer,* September 1913

speck above the horizon. It seemed to have claimed the attention of the inhabitants of the air first, many birds being much perturbed in the vicinity of Dundalk Bay. Soon the airman was steering his course up the bay taking practically the same line as a ship entering harbour would have taken."[26]

Dawes first attempt at landing was aborted as he was too close to a boundary fence and also some horses had to be removed from the field. He took the opportunity to circle the town and as he did so the crowd began to gather. The *Examiner's* report continued:

"This time he came right over the fence and alighted in quite a central position with a precision and smoothness that evoked much favourable comment. This was Dundalk's first experience of the landing of an aeroplane."[27]

A BE2a of No 2 Squadron prepares for take-off. *(No 2 Squadron Archive)*

Dawes was greeted by Lieutenant Studhert of the RFA. He commented that he had maintained a height of 3000 feet and had covered some 65 miles in about an hour. During the course of the evening many local people took the opportunity to visit the barrack grounds and view the aeroplane. About 3000 gathered the following afternoon to watch the departure:

"After running a short distance along the field the machine gracefully and gradually ascended. The spectators cheered enthusiastically but in a few minutes the aeroplane was lost to sight."[28]

The *Irish Times* described the arrangements made for the airmen:

"The Royal Flying Corps camp at Rathbane presents a very picturesque appearance. Hangars for seven aeroplanes have been erected and also tents for the officers, 17 in number and the 80 rank and file. The advance party under the supervision of Lieutenant Harvey have completed their work."[29]

The ground support equipment had travelled by sea and consisted of portable canvas hangars, spare engines, wings, stores, tools and other spares. These were conveyed by means of five lorries, six cars and six motor bicycles. A forty-acre field had been reserved for use

---

26  *Dundalk Examiner,* September 1913
27  Ibid
28  Ibid
29  The *Irish Times,* September 1913

as a base camp for the aircraft, while the officers enjoyed the comforts of Cruise's Royal Hotel. The arrivals caused something of a sensation in Limerick on the evening of 1 September:

"Two of which had overflown the city before they steered for the camp at Rathbane, where a hearty reception was given to the aeronauts on their arrival by the troops and the constabulary in the camps and by the numbers of the public who walked, motored, and cycled there."[30]

Some of No 2 Squadron's ground crew with their transport and stores at Rathbane in September 1913. *(Brendan Treacy Collection)*

On Tuesday, 2 September the Maurice Farman, No 207, Captain Dawes and Lieutenant Harvey, flew the 50 miles from Limerick towards Birr in King's County (now Offaly) for the purpose of selecting a suitable landing ground and would have alighted in the Fourteen Acres of Birr Barracks (the Depot of the Leinster Regiment) but for the fact that sheep were grazing there and so obstructing a safe landing. The *Midland Tribune* stated that:

"The aeroplane was first seen by officials at the railway and was then between the Birr Military Barracks and the station and was flying low. The two men seated in the machine could be seen quite distinctly. The buzzing of the engine attracted the attention of a number of people on the street in the immediate vicinity of the station. The aeroplane was first seen at 11.40 o'clock."[31]

The *King's County Chronicle* commented:

"This field is not altogether suitable as it is on the small side, while the Thirty Acres below has a slope. The biplane was seen by a good many people before it left in the direction of Roscrea. When it got as far as Sharavogue (just a few miles south of Birr), it circled a couple of times and landed in one of the Earl of Huntingdon's fields between the polo ground and the railroad."[32]

Unfortunately a gust of wind caught the Farman, the right wing tip touched the ground first and caused an interplane strut to break. This proved something of a bonus for the crowd of onlookers who gathered, as they had much more time to inspect the novelty. As luck would have it, the annual tournament of the King's County Polo Club was being held that week, contested by the 'Wasps', 'Midges', 'Moths', 'Bees' and 'Butterflies'. A telegram

30  *Limerick Leader,* September 1913
31  *Midland Tribune,* 6 September 1913
32  *King's County Chronicle,* 4 September 1913

On his way to Limerick, Lieutenant Waldron landed at the Curragh to refuel and returned there to visit friends for lunch two days later. *(via Sergeant Wayne Fitzgerald)*

summoned a mechanic from Rathbane, who arrived by motor vehicle at 5.30 pm. Repairs were effected within 20 minutes and the two airmen (pilot and observer) prepared to depart:

> "The aeroplane ran rapidly along the field for four or five hundred yards and then rising over 'mother earth' was bidden adieu by loud cheers. It soared over the trees and in a few minutes came back at a fairly high altitude right over the field where it had met with the mishap, and heading for Limerick was eagerly watched till it was a mere speck in the sky and finally disappeared."[33]

It is also thought that Ferdy Waldron took the opportunity to visit his friends at the Curragh for lunch, before the start of the manoeuvres. The *Limerick Leader* noted that on 3 September:

> "A number of exhibition flights were given today at Rathbane, being much appreciated by the crowds of people present as a number of the machines circled over the city and their graceful flights at a height of hundreds of feet were watched with great interest."[34]

The final arrival was McLean in No 272 who flew in on Friday, 5 September. Longcroft soon made his mark with the local public, as the press reported on:

---

33  Ibid
34  *Limerick Leader,* September 1913

At Rathbane, seated in the BE2a is Captain Longcroft, standing is Lieutenant Waldron. *(No 2 Squadron Archive)*

"The spiral descents of the Flight Commander, Captain Longcroft, being a new experience to most of the 8000 people who went out from Limerick to witness the event."[35]

More excitement was to follow on Saturday 6th,

"Three BE Biplanes arrived in Birr on Saturday from Limerick. They executed manoeuvres over the town, and the people were afforded a fine view of the machines as they made graceful turns and swoops high in the air. The biplanes descended in the Fourteen Acres, Crinkle, around which an interested crowd remained all day. The pilots of the machines were Captain Becke, Captain Longcroft, Lieutenant Waldron, Reserve Captain Tucker, Lieutenant Todd and Lieutenant Martin. Mechanics arrived by motors later in the day. The biplanes remained at Fourteen Acres until Monday morning. So interested are all in the aeroplanes, that even the Board of Guardians, including their popular clerk, deserted their posts on hearing the cry of aeroplane. After watching the machines out of sight they returned to their work."[36]

There were many extra soldiers in Birr that Saturday, whose patronage was welcomed by the local shopkeepers with the result that:

---

35  Ibid
36  *Midland Tribune,* 13 September 1913

"It was almost impossible to get butter or eggs at Saturday's market, as all available supplies had been bought for the troops."[37]

On 8 September, Captain Longcroft, en-route from Rathbane to the Curragh, in BE2 No 218, attempted to make a landing in a field owned by Mr J Gleeson of Rose Cottage, Brosna, a village in the south-western corner of King's County,

"On coming to the ground it landed in a hole, smashing some of the struts. It continued to run along, and got into a ditch, where further damage was done. The machine was dismantled on Tuesday and taken to Limerick on Wednesday. No one was hurt."[38]

The damage was quite severe as the undercarriage was torn off and about a foot from the tip of each propeller blade.

More than 20,000 troops were involved in the exercises over the counties of Limerick, Tipperary and Kilkenny, divided into the 'Brown Army' (the 5th Division, commanded by Major General Sir Charles Fergusson) and the 'White Army' (the 6th Division, commanded by Major General William Pulteney). The War Office communication to the press concerning the RFC's participation commented on the challenges ahead:

"Owing to the difficult nature of the country there are certain to be sufficient casualties amongst the aircraft for the practice of repair, replacement etc. It is

BE2a of No 2 Squadron, Serial No 218. *(No 2 Squadron Archive)*

37  Ibid
38  Ibid

expected that numerous interesting experiments will be carried out by the leaders on both sides with the object of deceiving observers in aircraft."[39]

Aircraft were allocated to each side. The minimum allowable height was 3000 feet. To ensure that this rule was kept a barograph was installed on each aircraft and inspected by the umpires. Flight lower than the minimum was disallowed for reconnaissance purposes, it was deemed to be vulnerable to ground fire, which showed a certain faith in the musketry of the ground troops. A contemporary report in the *Irish Times* from the 'battlefield' stated of the major exercise on 16 September:

"During the early stages of the fight, the airmen of both sides were constantly in flight. The amount of information the observers in these machines were able to convey to their respective generals either directly or by means of messages dropped from the dizzy heights to units of the force was most valuable. All the while the machines went steadily and fortunately without any accident to their intrepid pilots and observers."[40]

The conditions were challenging as the weather was rarely very pleasant, the *Irish Times* commenting:

"Having regard to the inclement weather and the high wind that prevailed it seemed incredible that any person would venture aloft in an aeroplane on a day like this."[41]

---

39  The *Irish Times,* September 1913
40  Ibid
41  Ibid

BE2a in flight near
Rathbane. *(No 2
Squadron Archive)*

The *Midland Tribune* also described progress at the manoeuvres, noting that the 5th Division was encamped at Roscrea and that severe 'fighting' had taken place around Shinrone, adding:

"The aeroplanes seem to be about the best value of the lot – at least they are the most talked about. Some of them have been down, and more of them up, and some have got into difficulties. The aeroplanes seem to have an infirmary of their own. When one of them gets injured a motor aeroplane ambulance comes along and takes the injured plane off to Limerick for repairs. There was a lot of talk in Birr during the week about hangars being out up at the Fourteen Acres. Disappointment was felt when the scheme did not fructify. All are glad that none of the airmen, so far, at least, have come to grief. They go up with a laugh, taking their seats in the machine with as much sang froid as one would in an ordinary car."[42]

The *King's County Chronicle* of 18 September included an interesting short article which is reproduced here in full:

"The excitement created in Roscrea, Birr and other parts of the Midlands by the appearance for the first time of aeroplanes flying over these towns been universal among the public of all ages from the little child to the old man and woman. On Thursday [11th] owing to a petrol tube leaking, No 217 alighted in a stubble field near Knockshegowna, and in a short time several spectators were on the spot. Dr Houlihan, who had his motor, brought Captain Becke to a blacksmith and later in the evening the mechanical bird left.

On Saturday [13th] three biplanes of the BE or all-British type, visited Birr, two of them circling over the town to the wonder of hundreds of country people at the markets. The first to come, No 218, was in charge of Captain Longcroft, one of the most intrepid officers of the Royal Flying Corps. Some time afterwards came Captain Becke on No 217, and later Lieutenant Waldron arrived on No 273. The last mentioned machine we believe is the one which secured the prize for the greatest altitude in the British Isles. Three officers, as reserves, were Captain Tucker and Lieutenants Todd and Martyn.

The aeroplanes remained till Monday morning in the spacious field near the military barrack known as Hector's field and were guarded by 25 police from Limerick. The biplanes are of a different make to the one which recently had the mishap at Sharavogue. This was a French machine, a Maurice Farman, and is the

---

42  *Midland Tribune*, 13 September 1913

BE2a No 217 at Rathbane. *(Brendan Treacy Collection)*

only one of the kind employed in the manoeuvres. In another column we append intelligence calculated to arouse amazement at the fearless courage of the men who go up in these new craft.[43]

A good description of how the aircraft went about their task stated:

> "The work of the aeroplanes was a notable feature of the operations, and from one of the biplanes a message dropped among the ranks of the 16th Lancers. It is interesting to note how these are conveyed. The message is placed in a weighted bag from which coloured streamers flow. The bag contains a request that the finder will forward it to the Divisional Headquarters."[44]

Some idea of the hazardous nature of flying in those days can be gained from the fact that Royal Army Medical Corps personnel attended all anticipated landings. The value of the aeroplanes had been proven to be very useful and was compared favourably to the time, manpower and effort in effecting a similar return from the cavalry. The flight of 400 miles from Montrose to Limerick had been a considerable challenge, while during the manoeuvres each machine had flown some 2000 miles in an area which was exceptionally bad from an aviation point of view, owing to the scarcity of landing grounds, inclement weather (mist and rain), as well as the principal operations taking place in a mountain defile. There were no cases of engine failure and no machines landed in 'hostile territory'.[45]

43  *King's County Chronicle,* 18 September 1913
44  *King's County Chronicle,* 25 September 1913
45  Air1/687/21/20/2 History of 2 Sqn

After taking part in the exercises preparations were made to return home at the end of the month. The return journey was not without incident. The fate of Maurice Farman No 207 is not completely clear. JM Bruce notes that it was extensively damaged at Ballyhornan, Co Down on 24 September but this may be confusing it with the fate of BE2 No 273 (see below).[46] The *Midland Tribune* adds further information:

> "Five or six aeroplanes passed over Roscrea on Tuesday [23rd], on their way from Limerick after the Manoeuvres. The first to arrive was Captain Dawes [in 207?] and he was the only one to have trouble. He descended owing to petrol troubles, in a field belonging to Mr Bergin, at Cooleshall, at about 11 o'clock in the morning. Having procured a further petrol supply from the town, and was in the act of starting, he damaged the machine, and a mechanic bad to be sent for to Limerick. At 9.30 on Wednesday morning he restarted with his passenger. The weather be pronounced bad for flying, and unfortunately be seems to have had further mishaps at the Curragh. A large crowd of 3,000 or 4,000 people assembled to view the start, while as the time was not very well known, anxious watchers assembled at an early hour of the morning. One of the first to arrive – at about 5.30, we are told – was a signalman employed at Ballybrophy, but as he had to be on duty at eight at the station, he had to return home disappointed. During the night, and all the time the biplane remained in the place it was guarded by the police."[47]

In any event it did not apparently return to Montrose. Meanwhile four BE2s, flown by Longcroft (No 218), McLean (No 272), L Dawes (No 225) and Lieutenant RB Martyn departed from Limerick at 10.30 am on 23 September, landing at the Curragh an hour later for a leisurely lunch and taking off again at 3.00 pm for Newcastle, Co Down, where they arrived at 4.15 pm. The first three named landed near Bryansford, while Martyn alighted at Dundrum. The purpose of breaking the journey here was to re-attach the floatation gear in advance of the sea crossing. On the morning of 24 September Longcroft took off again but decided that the wind was too fresh and landed on the beach near to the clubhouse of the Royal County Down Golf Club, where the three airmen were 'royally entertained'[48] to lunch. Martyn in No 273 was not so affected by the weather and was able to resume his journey – which unluckily was soon terminated by engine trouble at Ballyhornan which was near Ardglass. The resultant forced landing caused such extensive damage that a breakdown party had to drive from Limerick to load the aircraft onto their lorry for shipment home.

Captain Becke, flying No 217, who was travelling independently from the main group, also had engine problems and landed in Co Meath much to the delight of spectators who rushed to the spot from far and near. A policeman from Bohermeen Barracks was on patrol near the scene and soon a wire was despatched to the head-constable at Navan. The Royal

46  *Britain's First Warplanes* by JM Bruce, Arms and Armour Press, Poole 1987
47  *Midland Tribune*, 27 September 1913
48  *Down Recorder*, September 1913

Captain Becke and
BE2a No 217 near Kells,
Co Meath. *(Author's
Collection)*

Irish Constabulary took charge, mounting a guard and erecting a fence until a repair crew (also summoned by telegram) arrived to change the engine, which had suffered a broken bearing. Becke rested in the comfort of the Headfort Arms in Kells and was able to resume his journey on 25 September, encountering strong southerly winds and banks of fog as he crossed the Irish coast but nevertheless reaching Cults Farm that afternoon. He spent the night at Loch Inch Castle as the guest of the Earl of Stair.

Longcroft and his two companions were staying most comfortably in the Slieve Donard Hotel waiting for the weather to improve. On the evening of 25 September Longcroft made a 20 minute flight, bringing the aircraft from its sheltered position on the golf links and taking off from the beach in very blustery conditions:

> "He flew slowly and under 1000 feet at first but after making several sweeps round the country between Newcastle, Dundrum and Castlewellan, he rose to a very considerable elevation and was almost lost to view in the clouds over Slieve Donard. The daring aviator continued to fly high and appeared merely a speck in the sky. He next flew seawards and then suddenly made a magnificent spiral descent."[49]

This was much to the appreciation of hundreds of onlookers and also of the *Down Recorder's* correspondent who concluded his report:

> "One is proud to take off his hat to the gallant pilots who carry their lives in their hands every moment that they are in the air.[50]

---

49 Ibid
50 Ibid

On 26 September, the weather being clear and calm, they were able to fly back to Scotland. On the way across the North Channel the three BEs flew into heavy fog which became appreciably lighter as they crossed the Wigtownshire coast. Longcroft landed safely at Cults Farm but McLean so lost his bearings that he landed in a bog near Troon, some 50 miles to the north. The aircraft was recovered and flew again. Leonard Dawes also got lost but was able to land safely twice before joining Longcroft and Becke. Later that afternoon all three had reached Montrose.

At the conclusion of the manoeuvres Patrick Joseph Aherne, Late Sergeant Major 1st Leinster Regiment, wrote from his home in Birr a detailed analysis, which included the following prescient thoughts:

> "The part played by aviation calls for a word on its effect on the conditions of modern warfare. Will the same conditions prevail amongst air belligerents as exist with fighting bodies on terra firma? Will they endeavour to destroy or capture each other? Or will aviators be non-combatants? Not the latter certainly. The deduction, therefore, is that the army which possesses the best and most up-to-date aeroplanes and dirigibles [airships] in the next war will have incalculable advantages over others not so provided."[51]

All in all No 2 Squadron's visit to Ireland may indeed be regarded as a highly important and successful dress rehearsal for the operational deployment of the Royal Flying Corps to France just under a year later. This was a very noteworthy feat for those early days, crossing the short stretch of sea between Scotland and Ireland twice in rudimentary flying machines with a 70 hp (52 kW) engine and a top speed of between 50 and 70 mph (80 to 112 kph) was not a challenge for the faint-hearted. It was also a considerable technical achievement for the pilots, mechanics and riggers – the aircraft having flown an average of 2000 miles (3200 km) each over the period.

Captain Dawes later commanded No 11 Squadron on the Western Front in 1915. He rose to the rank of Colonel, ending the war in the Balkans as the Commanding Officer of the RAF forces there. He retired the following year with the rank of Wing Commander and served again in that rank for the duration of the Second World War. He died in 1960 at the age of 80. Captain Becke (1879–1949), Notts and Derby Regiment, became a Group Captain before he retired in 1920, with the honorary rank of Brigadier General. Captain Longcroft (1883–1958), who had originally joined the Welch Regiment, attained the rank of Air Vice Marshal before he retired in 1929. All three were awarded the DSO. Lieutenant Waldron who was born in 1887, had first served as a cavalryman with the 19th Hussars, was a Major and commanding No 60 Squadron when he was shot down and killed over Cambrai on 3 July 1916. Lieutenant McLean (1883–1970), Royal Scots, rose to command Numbers 5 and 8 Squadrons and later became a Lieutenant Colonel and Commandant of the Central Flying School. Lieutenant Leonard Dawes, late of the Middlesex Regiment, who was not

---

51  *King's County Chronicle,* 25 September 1913

related to George, commanded No 29 Squadron on its formation as the third single-seater scout squadron equipped with DH2s. RB Martyn, Wiltshire Regiment, commanded No 22 Squadron in 1916 and was awarded the MC in 1917. Concerning the aircraft, No 207 did not fly again but all the BE2s flew on into 1914 (with the possible exception of No 273). As for No 2 Squadron, it would return to Ireland again in 1920, but that is another story.

A DH2, as flown by
No 29 Squadron.
*(Author's Collection)*

Chapter 6

# The Last Days before the War: 1914

## Henri Salmet and FP Raynham

In June 1914, Henri Salmet (by than the Chief Instructor at the Blériot Flying School at Hendon) returned to Ulster with FP Raynham (1893–1954) (the AV Roe test pilot, RAeC Certificate No 85, May 9, 1911), flying two aircraft, a 80 hp (59 kW) Blériot XI-2 and an Avro 504 floatplane – the prototype of this famous aircraft which had been purchased by the *Daily Mail* and fitted with interchangeable floats for a nationwide tour. They displayed them at several locations, including Bangor, Lurgan and Warrenpoint. The event in Bangor was in the hands of the local council and took place on 18 June. Special trains were laid on, steamers brought further spectators along the coast from Belfast and local schoolchildren were treated to a half-day holiday. Flying took place from the beach at this popular seaside resort, among those taking the opportunity to fly with Salmet were the wife of the MP for East Belfast and RL (Bobby) Dunville, one of John Dunville's three sons. *Flight* magazine reported that in Lurgan:

*Below:* FP Raynham with an Avro biplane. *(Author's Collection)*

*Below right:* Mr Salmet the Daily Mail Aviator. *(via Terry Mace)*

> "Raynham started from a small pond while Salmet flew from an adjoining field. In spite of the fact that the whole place was surrounded by trees, making it difficult to get out, both pilots carried a good many passengers during the day."[1]

1 *Flight,* 26 June 1914

They then flew 25 miles (40 km) to Warrenpoint, billed in the press as "the popular Co Down health resort"[2] and which would also be providing a number of other entertainments and attractions, including military band performances and illuminations. As was often the case, special trains were laid on at reduced fares:

> "Raynham followed the canal from Portadown and took exactly an hour, but during half the journey his motor was only firing on five cylinders and he flew low down between the hills; there was also a strong wind blowing."[3]

At Warrenpoint Salmet flew from the Golf Links and Raynham from the Bay, flying over the Carlingford Mountains. One of Raynham's passengers was Master Lex Fisher, aged 6½, the son of a local solicitor, who thoroughly enjoyed his flight and wanted to go up again. A proposed extension of the tour to Bray sadly did not take place, reportedly for financial reasons.

On 28 June the assassination of the Austrian Archduke Franz Ferdinand and his wife in Sarajevo, set events in motion which would change the lives of millions of people. After the outbreak of war, Salmet joined the Aéronautique Militaire (French Army Air Service), and served in the non-commissioned rank of Maréchal des Logis, with Escadrille C9,

*Salmet and his Blériot at Ballyholme, Bangor in 1914. (BELUM.Y.W.05.15.57 © National Museums Northern Ireland, Collection Ulster Museum)*

---

2 *Irish Independent,* 6 June 1914
3 Ibid

Raynham's Avro 504
at Warrenpoint in
1914. *(Ernie Cromie
Collection)*

A Caudron G.4 with two
80 hp (59.6 kW) Rhone
engines. *(Author's
Collection)*

flying Caudron G.4 reconnaissance bombers from Villers-lès-Nancy. On 7 April 1915, he was awarded the Croix de Guerre. He survived the war but his eventual fate is not known. Raynham had a successful career as a test pilot flying Avro, Sopwith, Martinsyde and Hawker aircraft. He spent much of the inter-war years in India. During the Second World War he worked for the Air Ministry and died suddenly in 1954 while on a caravan tour of the USA with his wife.

## Lord Carbery

One of the most remarkable figures to grace Irish skies was Josh C Evans-Freke, Lord Carbery, (1892–1970) who gained his Aviators' Certificate in France on 2 September 1913, had made a name for himself in air races in England and Europe, including the second Schneider Trophy speed contest in April 1914 and the third Aerial Derby in June of the same year. His family seat was in Co Cork at Castle Freke, where succeeded to the title in 1898 and grew up in comfortable circumstances. He had gained a reputation for wild behaviour from boyhood. At the age of eight placed an apple on the head of a gardener and shot it off with an air pistol. He also shot the hat off the head of a poacher in the castle grounds, slightly grazing his head; the hat, complete with bullet hole, has been preserved. At fourteen he went secretly to Cork and arrived back driving his first motor car.

He came home to Ireland in 1914, where he made several flights in and around Cork City in his 80 hp (59 kW) Morane-Saulnier monoplane, a

Lord Carbery and his Morane-Saulnier. *(Author's Collection)*

much more capable aircraft when compared with the Blériots, Deperdussin, Handley Page or Farmans used by other showmen. Carbery also performed the first loop-the-loop in Ireland at the Clonakilty Agricultural Society's annual show on 5 July. The basic charge for a flight was £5, with a loop included the tariff rose to £25. On 9 July one of his passengers, Miss LE Townsend of Lislenane, Clonakilty, could claim to have been the first lady in Ireland to take part in a public flying exhibition. The *Cork Examiner* reported:

"Amidst breathless silence, the machine darted forward, it ran along the ground for about fifty yards and then slowly and very gradually rose in the air against a fairly strong south-west breeze. As the machine neared the boundary of the grounds, the crowd became tremulous with fear for the safety of the aviator as it appeared as if he and his machine would collide with the corrugated iron fence. The suspense was

Lord Carbery comes in to land his Morane. *(via Terry Mace)*

only momentary, however, for the machine rose sharply and gracefully amidst the loud cheers of the crowd. Having performed two loops he then executed the 'falling leaf' descent before flying away."[4]

He was married to José Metcalfe (1894–1977), a spectacularly beautiful young woman, the daughter of Major 'Jumbo' Metcalfe, from an acceptable military background, but not a brilliant one. José was with John when, on 9 July 1914, Cork 'Aviation Day', he gave an aeronautical exhibition over the city and then landed his Morane on the University athletic grounds at the Mardyke. The *Cork Examiner* described how:

"He took his seat in the machine. His mechanic turned the propeller and the engine went to work right away, its eight cylinders emitting an artillery-like roar. Immediately on the machine getting clear, Lord Carbery put the monoplane in motion and ran it a short distance when it ascended at a very narrow angle to the ground, so narrow indeed that the uninitiated (and most of those present were uninitiated) believed that it would go straight to the football posts. However, when about 30 yards from the posts, the aviator cleverly changed the steering of his machine giving it an extraordinary angle to the ground so much so that it was almost perpendicular. In this manner it ascended swiftly and sharply and still rising it headed off in a north westerly direction."[5]

Carbery's Morane at a display on 17 July 1914. *(Author's Collection)*

---

4  *Cork Examiner,* July 1914
5  Ibid

LORD CARBERY.

University Football Grounds.

THURSDAY, 9th JULY, 1914.

John Carbery gave other displays over Bandon and Beaumont Park, Blackrock, where one of his passengers was Master Gerald Cobb, who was just 11 years old. "The people of the district," reported the *Cork Examiner*, would have "an opportunity of witnessing the daring and youthful aviator performing in the air feats which it would be impossible to describe, and must be seen to be believed." And it later reported that there were "shrieks and gasps of terror" when "the noble Lord looped the loop over the crowd." Towards the end of the display, José went up with her husband. She was wearing a "tight fitting dark cap". Although said by some to be looking rather pale, "she evidently enjoyed the prospect of looping the loop."[6]

*Above left:* Lord Carbery and his mechanic at the Mardyke in 1914. *(Author's Collection)*

*Above:* A poster for Lord Carbery's appearance at Cork's 'Aviation Day' in July 1914. *(Author's Collection)*

*Flight* magazine reported briefly on Carbery's activities in Ireland and gives an indication of just how much pilots and aircraft had advanced in a few short years:

> "During the last fortnight Lord Carbery has been giving several exhibitions in Ireland on his 80 hp Morane-Saulnier. On Wednesday 15th July he was in Waterford in connection with the Agricultural Show there. The wind was rather troublesome, but he nevertheless put up several displays of looping, turnovers, tail slides &c, with and without passengers."[7]

One of his passengers in Waterford was a reporter from the *Irish Times*:

> "Without overcoat, hat or even goggles, Lord Carbery climbed into the aeroplane and I followed him. No sooner had we strapped in than we were off. There were a couple of jolts as the machine sped along the ground but in a moment or two it rose in the air. It swayed from side to side, then tossed backwards and forwards, and one

6  Ibid
7  *Flight*, 24 July 1914

had the feeling of being in a boat in decidedly bad weather. When I looked around we were several hundred feet up. There was a magnificent view of the surrounding district, the River Suir winding its way through the countryside before emptying itself into the sea, while the steamers in the river at Waterford appeared as mere model boats.

Presently Lord Carbery, making a megaphone of his hand, said, 'Terrific lot of wind, more than usually bad.' This was certainly encouraging news for me. Still I was enjoying my first real flight, my previous experience here with Mr Corbett Wilson last year having come to a disappointing end, the propeller breaking just as the machine left the ground. We were now going round in a circle, making a sharp spiral ascent. On one or two occasions as the machine banked, powerful squalls struck it and threatened to turn it over.

Presently Lord Carbery took what I thought at first was a watch out of his pocket and turning round showed it to me. 'Twenty-nine point something.' I read. One thousand, one hundred feet up was Lord Carbery's remark. With a wave of his hand Lord Carbery indicated that he was going to loop-the-loop. Next instant the machine shot rapidly upwards, went over on its back and in a moment or two came round to its normal position again. Looping the loop is quite a delightful experience."[8]

Carbery's next venue was Bray, whence his machine was taken by rail:

8 *Irish Times*, 15 July 1914

"Ascending early in the afternoon from the Cricket Ground in a series of spirals to a height of 3000 feet, passing the meanwhile over Bray Head, he executed several loops and tail slides. He then took up several passengers and caused some alarm by descending in a field outside. His reason for doing this was on account of the Cricket Ground being rather unsuitable for fast landing, and, moreover, somewhat unpleasantly crowded."[9]

He followed this before the end of the month with a flying visit to Powerscourt, featured in several photographs in the *Irish Independent* and a free exhibition in the grounds of Castle Bernard, the seat of the Earl of Bandon:

"After a circuit of the town Lord Carbery looped the loop twice, did the dead-leaf drop and other exhibition flying. On descending, he was given a most enthusiastic reception, and was presented with an address by the local branch of the Irish National Volunteers. Lady Carbery was presented with a handsome bouquet."[10]

In August further displays were given in Clonmel, Tralee Race Course and Youghal. Britain having declared war on Germany on 4 August, *Flight* noted that the remaining fixtures arranged had been cancelled, as Carbery, despite his strongly-held Nationalist political views, had offered his services to the Government.[11] This offer was accepted and during the Great War he served with courage and some distinction in the RNAS until September 1918, when he was honourably discharged, invalided due to wounds sustained in service.

It is undeniable, however, that Carbery had a most unusual personality. After the war he sold Castle Freke, but not before taking a shotgun to the family portraits. He spent some time in the USA, where his application for citizenship was refused because it was alleged that he had been involved in bootlegging prohibited alcoholic beverages. Not long afterwards he became one of the notorious Happy Valley Set in Kenya, changing his name by deed poll to John Evans Carbery. His personal life was no less controversial with allegations of marital cruelty and vicious rows with his several wives. Despite all of this he lived to a fairly ripe old age.

Lord Carbery and his Morane. *(via Terry Mace)*

9  *Flight,* 24 July 1914
10 *Flight,* 7 August 1914
11 *Flight,* 21 August 1914

## Conclusions

In the space of less than five years the public in Ireland had been able to see aeroplanes in more than 50 places, spread across 23 of the 32 counties. The performances given by the aviators had developed from short hops, straight flights and circuits to the thrilling aerobatic displays of Lord Carbery. A measure of the degree to which 'airmindedness' had taken told in Ireland may be taken from the work of the Irish aviation historian, Joe Gleeson. The results of his very detailed research in the National Archives, the Imperial War Museum and elsewhere have shown that no less than 6000 Irishmen joined the flying services during the Great War, at a cost of probably 500 casualties.

The outbreak of the Great War resulted in the Aero Club of Ireland being wound up after only five years, with its remaining funds being donated to the Red Cross.

There was still time for two Irishmen to make their mark before aerial hostilities were joined in earnest. The first to land in France on 13 August 1914 was an Anglo-Irishman, whose family hailed from Westmeath, Lieutenant HD Harvey-Kelly (1891–1917) (RAeC Certificate No 501, 30 May 1913) of No 2 Squadron, flying a BE2a from Dover to Amiens in one hour and 55 minutes. For his pains, he received a severe telling off from his squadron commander for having the temerity to arrive before him. Major CJ Burke (1881–1917), the youngest son of the Mr MCC Burke of Ballinhone House, Armagh, who was a massive, broad-shouldered, barrel-chested man, known behind his formidable back as 'Pregnant Percy'. He was respected for his courage, notorious for his rough landings and somewhat feared as a hard taskmaster. He learned to fly in France in a Farman biplane, gaining his Aéro-Club de France certificate No 260 in the process on 4 October 1910. He was a founding member of the Air Battalion, Royal Engineers in 1911 and then of the Royal Flying Corps in 1912.

*Right:* Lieutenant HD Harvey-Kelly. *(Author's Collection)*

*Far right:* Major Burke (right) and Captain Longcroft (left). *(Author's Collection)*

On 26 August 1914, Harvey-Kelly gained the first ever British victory in air-to-air combat despite flying an unarmed aircraft, forcing his opponent to land by his aggressive flying. Having chased off the crew he set fire to the German Taube and took off. 'Bay' Harvey-Kelly was eventually shot down during 'Bloody April', having been promoted to Major and awarded the DSO. He died of head wounds in a German hospital. By this time Lieutenant Colonel Burke DSO was also dead. In the summer of 1916 Burke rejoined his old regiment, the Royal Irish, which was suffering a severe shortage of officers. He was killed in action on 9 April 1917, the first day of the Battle of Arras, while commanding a battalion of the East Lancashire Regiment.

During the course of the First World War, the aeroplane was transformed from a novelty into a practical machine capable of transporting men, fuel, bombs and guns. Thoughts turned, even while the war was still in progress, to using this lifting capacity for commercial purposes. As is still the case today, the stretch of water separating Ireland from Great Britain presented both a challenge and an opportunity.

Over this brief period the airmen described above, with a mixture of daring, panache, skill and luck, had written an indelible chapter in the aviation history of Ireland.

Standing far left, Lieutenant Harvey-Kelly; seated second left, Captain G Dawes; next left Major Burke; then Lieutenants Waldron and Dawes. (Author's Collection)

# Appendix

THE ON-LINE RESOURCES *Black's Guide to Ireland 1906*, from Archive.org, *Atlas and Cyclopedia of Ireland 1900* and *Belfast and Ulster Towns Directory 1910* both from Library Ireland, give a fascinating snapshot of Ireland over a century ago.

Its population of 4.3 million was spread between the four provinces as follows: Leinster, to the east, 1.1m, Munster, in the south and west, 1.0m, Connaught, to the far west, 0.6m and Ulster, in the north, 1.5m. Dublin was the largest city with a population of 250,000, followed by Belfast with 208,000. Of the other major cities and towns mentioned in this book, the next largest was Cork with 80,124 "the chief trading and commercial city of the southern half of Ireland", Limerick had over 38,500 inhabitants, while Waterford had 22,500. Newry, "a thriving market town 43 miles from Belfast, a parliamentary borough and an important port for agricultural produce and cattle", Dundalk (just over halfway between Belfast and Dublin) and Lurgan, "a damask and linen weaving town 20 miles from Belfast", all had populations between 11,000 and 12,000. Bangor and Newtownards both had in excess of 8000, while Enniscorthy, Banbridge, "a good business town", Birr, Larne and Mullingar, "a busy agricultural market town and angling centre"; all hovered around the 5000 mark. Next came Castlebar, "the county town of Mayo and the residence of the Earl of Lucan", Clonakilty, Cavan, "in the midst of very fertile country", Ballymoney, "one of the most thriving market towns in Co Antrim", Tuam, "a well-to-do and prosperous town", Roscrea, Kells and Maryborough with between 2800 and 3800. Antrim, Warrenpoint, "a sea bathing resort beautifully situated in Carlingford Bay" and Newcastle, "a charming seaport and bathing resort" were much smaller, with less than 2000 apiece.

The charming village of Hillsborough, the birthplace of aviation in Ireland, was recorded as having just 671 inhabitants.

A contemporary advert for Arthur Blake's business. He designed and constructed a monoplane late in 1909 (see pg 34). *(Larne Museum & Arts Centre)*

# References

## Books and Journals

Baring, Maurice, *Flying Corps Headquarters 1914–1918* (London 1920)

Best, Simon, *Frontiers A Colonial Dynasty* (Aotearoa 2013)

Brown, Timothy C, *Flying with the Larks* (Stroud 2013)

Brett, R Dallas, *History of British Aviation 1908–1914* (London 1933)

Bruce, Gordon, *John D Dunville Aeronaut* (unpublished manuscript Belfast 1978)

Bruce, JM, *Britain's First Warplanes* (Poole 1987)

Byrne, Liam, *History of Aviation in Ireland* (Dublin 1980)

Clarke, Michael, with Woods, Jack, *Harry Ferguson – Before the Plough* (Donaghadee 2009)

Connon, Peter, *In the Shadow of the Eagle's Wings – Aviation in Cumbria 1825–1914* (Penrith 1982)

Corlett, John, *Aviation in Ulster* (Belfast 1981)

Cummins, Patrick J, *Corbett Wilson- Aviation Pioneer* (Old Waterford Society, Decies XXXV Summer 1987)

Curtis, Joe, *Castlebar* (Dublin 2013)

Fennelly, Teddy, *Fitz – and the Famous Flight* (Portlaoise 1997)

Foxrock Local History Club, *Foxrock Miscellany* (Dublin 2012)

Gleeson, Joe, *Irish Aviators of World War I* (Dublin 2012)

Gollin, Alfred M, *The Impact of Air Power on the British People and Their Government 1909–14* (Stanford 1989)

Gray J, with Beck C and Roberts, Sqn Ldr SR, *Birth of Aviation in Northern Ireland* (Unpublished manuscript)

Harper, Harry, *Ace Air Reporter* (London 1944)

Hayes, KE, *A History of the RAF and USNAS in Ireland 1913–1923* (Dublin 1988)

Hume, Dr David, *People of the Lough Shore – A Memoir of Past Lives and Bygone Times from Ballycarry, Glynn, Islandmagee, Magheramorne and Whitehead 1790–1950* (Trafford 2007)

Hurren BJ, *The Fellowship of the Air* (London 1951)

Hywel, William, *Modest Millionaire* (Denbigh 1973)

MacCarron, Donal, *A View from Above* (Dublin 2000)

MacCarron, Donal, *Letters from an Early Bird* (Barnsley 2006)

Montgomery, Bob, *Early Aviation in Ireland* (Tankardstown 2013)

Munson, Kenneth, *Pioneer Aircraft 1903–14* (London 1969)

O'Drisceoil, Donal and O'Drisceoil, Diarmuid, *Fifty Years Have Flown: The History of Cork Airport* (Dublin 2011)

O'Giolláin, Brigadier General Seamus, *Curragh 90th Anniversary Handover* (Irish Defence Forces 2012)

O'Rourke, Madeleine, *Air Spectaculars – Air Displays in Ireland* (Dublin 1998)

Pixton, Stella, *Howard Pixton* (Barnsley 2014)

Pudney, John, *Bristol Fashion* (London 1960)

Skelton, Marvin L, *Captain Dawes and 2 Squadron RFC prepare for war* (Cross and Cockade Vol 23 No 4 1992)

Skelton, Marvin L, *GWP Dawes: The Early Years* (Unpublished manuscript)

Sprigg, T and Stanhope Thompson, AJ, *Who's Who in British Aviation 1932* (London 1932)

Sykes, Major General Sir Frederick, *From Many Angles* (London 1942)

## National Archive

Air1/802/204/4/1119, Air1/687/21/20/2

## Newspapers

| | |
|---|---|
| *Aberdeen Evening Express* | *Mayo News* |
| *Ballymena Observer* | *Midland Reporter* |
| *Ballymena Weekly Telegraph* | *Midland Tribune* |
| *Belfast Evening Telegraph* | *Munster Express* |
| *Belfast News Letter* | *New York Times* |
| *Connaught Telegraph* | *Newtownards Chronicle* |
| *Donegal News* | *North Devon Journal* |
| *Down Recorder* | *Northern Constitution* |
| *Dundalk Examiner* | *Northern Whig* |
| *Evening Herald* | *Skibbereen Eagle* |
| *Flight* | *Somerset and West of England Advertiser* |
| *Freeman's Journal* | *Southern Star* |
| *Irish Examiner* | *The Aero* |
| *Irish Independent* | *The Aeronautical Journal* |
| *Irish Press* | *The Aeroplane* |
| *Irish Times* | *The Frontier Sentinel* |
| *Kildare Observer* | *The Mercury* |
| *King's County Chronicle* | *The Nation* |
| *Larne Weekly Telegraph* | *The Newry Reporter* |
| *Leinster Express* | *The Times* |
| *Limerick Leader* | *Tuam Herald* |
| *Liverpool Daily Post* | *Westmeath Examiner* |

## Websites

www.apw.airwar1.org.uk

https://archive.org/details/blacksguidetoire00adam (Black's Guide to Ireland 1906)

www.boards.ancestry.co.uk

www.davidandkay.me.uk

www.flightglobal.com

www.gracesguide.co.uk

www.harryfergusonlegacy.com

www.irishnewsarchive.com

www.libraryireland.com/Atlas/Home.php (Atlas and Cyclopedia of Ireland 1900)

www.libraryireland.com/UlsterDirectory1910/Contents.php (Belfast and Ulster Towns Directory 1910)

www.rafweb.org

www.thetimes.co.uk

www.twosqnassoc.co.uk/pages/stories/ghost/ghost.htm

www.writing.ie/tell-your-own-story/a-treasure-uncovered-in-east-sussex

## Acknowledgements

Keith Beattie (Ballymoney Museum), Brian Bowen (Handley Page Archive), Leanne Briggs (North Down Museum), Mark Brunel-Cohen, Carmel Byrne, Michael Byrne (Offaly Historical and Archaeological Society), Chris Cassidy (Heritage Officer, Newry Library), Michael Clarke, Gretta Connell (Westmeath County Library), Ian Craighead (The Rolls-Royce Heritage Trust), Ernie Cromie, Antoin Daltun, Mr & Mrs Harold W Dawes, Andrew Dawrent (Royal Aero Club), Peter Devitt (RAF Museum), Jason Diamond (Banbridge Tourism), John Doyle (Waterford Central Library), Glenn Dunne (National Library of Ireland), Teddy Fennelly, Sergeant Wayne Fitzgerald (Irish Defence Forces), Tracey Flynn (Carrick-on-Shannon Library), Dermot Foley (Dundalk Library), Justin Furlong (National Library of Ireland), Maud Hamill (Abbey Historical Society), Ivor Hamrock (Castlebar Library), Richard Hickey (Castlebar Library), Sinead Holland (Laois Library Services), Paul Hughes (*Westmeath Examiner*), Jackie Johnson, Tony Kearnes, John Kearney (Offaly Historical and Archaeological Society), Marian Kelso (Larne Museum), Maire Kennedy (Dublin City Library), Vincent Killowry (www.killowryart.com), Alan King (Castlebar Library), Gemma McLaughlin (*Ballymoney Chronicle*), John Lyons (Scouts NI), Terry Mace, John Maxwell, Anne Marie McAleese (Radio Ulster), Donal MacCarron, Captain Séan McCarthy (Irish Air Corps), Heather McGuicken (North Down Museum), Greag Mac an tSaoir (Newry Museum), Mary Petrina Mee (Galway Library), Berni Metcalfe (National Library of Ireland), Mandy Miles (Ferguson Family Museum), Alan Millar (*Ballymoney Chronicle*), Bob Montgomery (Hon Archivist Royal Irish Automobile Club), Ciara O'Brien (Wicklow Library), Paula O'Dornan (Athlone Library), Brian O'Loughlin (*Westmeath Examiner*), Michael O'Malley, Gilbert Ralph (Hon Archivist, Sir Henry Royce Foundation, Australia), Joe Rogers, Brendan Scott, Jonathan Smyth (Johnston Central Library, Cavan), Michael Swords, Tammy Travers, Michael Traynor, Hugo Wilhare.

# Index

## People

## Aeroplanes and Aerostats

## Places

## Miscellaneous: Bands, Clubs, Colleges, Companies, Regiments, Ships, Societies, Theatres, Units

# Author's Note

ONE OF THE PLEASURES of being a historian is that there is always something new to add to one's knowledge. By fortunate chance, just as this book was going to print, I learned about Co Tyrone's Edgar Harper. He was born in Dungannon in 1880 and was educated at Dungannon Royal School, Queen's University, Belfast, and Trinity College, Dublin. He became a lecturer in mathematics at Bangor University in Wales. While working there, he took particular interest in the mathematics of flight. In 1911, in conjunction with a colleague Allan Ferguson, he published his book, *Aerial Locomotion*, which was 'a popular account of the principles underlying the new science of aeronautics'[1].

He also contributed greatly to one of the seminal books on the theory of flight; GH Bryan's *Stability in Aviation*, which was also published in 1911.

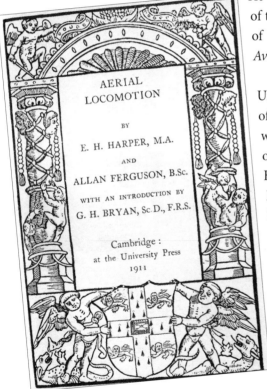

In 1913 Harper became Professor of Mathematical Physics at University College Cork. The future Prime Minister and President of Ireland, Éamon de Valera had also applied for the post but Harper was elected to the chair. Following the outbreak of war Harper obtained a commission with the 7th Royal Munster Fusiliers. He was later transferred to the 8th Battalion South Staffordshire Regiment, with whom he was promoted to Lieutenant. Harper's battalion took part in the Somme offensive, where he was killed in action on 10 July 1916, aged 36.[2]

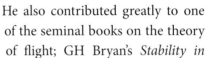

1 'One Hundred Years of GH Bryan's Stability in Aviation', *Journal of Aeronautical History*, Paper No 2011/4, TJM Boyd, Centre for Physics, University of Essex

2 See also *www.dungannonwardead.com*